FLORIDA

SCIENCE

Fusion

fusion [FYOO • zhuhn] a mixture or blend formed by fusing two or more things

This Interactive Student Edition belongs to

_____

Teacher/Room

_____

 HOUGHTON MIFFLIN HARCOURT

Consulting Authors

Michael A. DiSpezio
Global Educator
North Falmouth, Massachusetts

Marjorie Frank
Science Writer and Content-Area Reading
   Specialist
Brooklyn, New York

Michael Heithaus
Director, School of Environment and Society
Associate Professor, Department of Biological
   Sciences
Florida International University
North Miami, Florida

Donna Ogle
Professor of Reading and Language
National-Louis University
Chicago, Illinois

 HOUGHTON MIFFLIN HARCOURT

Front Cover: *green anole* ©Jeremy Woodhouse/Photodisc/Getty Images; *prism* ©Larry Lilac/Alamy; *clownfish* ©Georgette Douwma/Photographer's Choice/Getty Images; *galaxy* ©Stocktrek/Corbis; *ferns* ©Mauro Fermariello/ Photo Researchers, Inc.

Back Cover: *robotic arm* ©Garry Gay/The Image Bank/Getty Images; *thermometer* ©StockImages/Alamy; *astronaut* ©NASA; *moth* ©Millard H. Sharp/Photo Researchers, Inc.

Printed in the U.S.A.

ISBN 978-0-547-36589-3

7 8 9 10 1421 19 18 17 16 15 14 13 12
4500344303   BCDEF

Program Advisors

Paul D. Asimow
*Professor of Geology and
    Geochemistry*
California Institute of Technology
Pasadena, California

Bobby Jeanpierre
*Associate Professor of Science
    Education*
University of Central Florida
Orlando, Florida

Gerald H. Krockover
*Professor of Earth and Atmospheric
    Science Education*
Purdue University
West Lafayette, Indiana

Rose Pringle
*Associate Professor
    School of Teaching and Learning*
College of Education
University of Florida
Gainesville, Florida

Carolyn Staudt
Curriculum Designer for Technology
KidSolve, Inc.
The Concord Consortium
Concord, Massachusetts

Larry Stookey
Science Department
Antigo High School
Antigo, Wisconsin

Carol J. Valenta
*Senior Vice President and Associate
    Director of the Museum*
Saint Louis Science Center
St. Louis, Missouri

Barry A. Van Deman
President and CEO
Museum of Life and Science
Durham, North Carolina

Florida Reviewers

Janet M. Acerra
Forest Lakes Elementary
Oldsmar, Florida

Shannan Combee
Inwood Elementary
Winter Haven, Florida

Amber J. Cooley
Jacksonville Heights Elementary
Jacksonville, Florida

Donna de la Paz
Trinity Oaks Elementary
New Port Richey, Florida

Nancy Carrier Duncan
Eustis Heights Elementary
Eustis, Florida

Marsha Dwyer
Kenwood K-8 Center
Miami, Florida

Jessica S. Fowler
Susie E. Tolbert Elementary
Jacksonville, Florida

Pat Houston
Northwood Elementary
Crestview, Florida

Timothy W. Peterson
Romeo Elementary
Dunnellon, Florida

Rosanne Phillips
Kenwood K-8 Center
Miami, Florida

Rose M. Sedely
Eustis Heights Elementary
Eustis, Florida

Gerilyn Stark-Jerry
Chain of Lakes Elementary
Winter Haven, Florida

Deborah S. Street
Southport Elementary
Southport, Florida

Janine Townsley
Norwood Elementary
Miami, Florida

Jessica Weiss
Westchase Elementary
Tampa, Florida

Power Up with Science Fusion!

Your program fuses . . .

Online Virtual Experiences

Hands-on Explorations

Active Reading

. . . to generate new science energy for today's science learner—you.

Active Reading

Be an active reader and make this book your own!

You can write your ideas, answer questions, draw graphs, make notes, and record your activity results right on these pages.

By the end of the school year, this book becomes a record of everything you learn in science.

Amph... or Rep...

How are amphibians and reptiles different?
Read on to learn about these two groups.

tive Reading As you read these two pages, draw circles around the words that signal when things are being compared.

Amphibians [am•FIB•ee•...

...Most amphibians have smooth, moist ...kin. Young amphibians have gills. ...ny adult amphibians have lungs. ...ptiles are animals with scales cov...ng their bodies. Lizards and tu...les are reptiles. Similar to amphibia...s, most reptiles hat... from eggs. A reptile b... lungs its wh... crocodiles, th... water must c...

...amphibian li... round water.

...rtle

...s reptile lays eggs.

Newts water.

Fril... Liza...

Frilled liza... lay their eg... the ground

Hands-on Explorations

Science is all about doing.

There are lots of exciting investigations on the Inquiry Flipchart.

Ask questions and test your ideas.

Draw conclusions and share what you learn.

Online Virtual Experiences

Explore cool labs and activities in the virtual world—where science comes alive and you make it happen.

What are the signs of a chemical change?

Photo taken first | Cannot tell
Cannot tell

Photo taken first | Photo taken last | Cannot tell

Drag your answers into position

signs of a chemical change?   HOUGHTON MIFFLIN HARCOURT

The Investigation Lab

analysis area

special screen   experiment area

evidence

you have a special screen that can help with your investigation. Now its time to get started!

See your science lessons from a completely different point of view—a digital point of view.

Science Fusion is new energy... just for YOU!

Contents

THE NATURE OF SCIENCE

EARTH AND SPACE SCIENCE

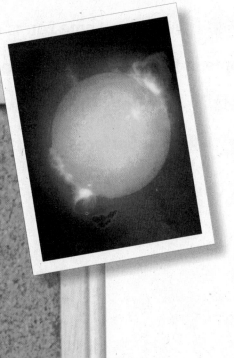

PHYSICAL SCIENCE

Unit 3—Properties of Matter

Big Idea 8

Properties of Matter

Big Idea 9

Changes in Matter

Unit 4—Forms of Energy

Big Idea 10

Forms of Energy

LIFE SCIENCE

Investigating Questions

Big Idea 1

The Practice of Science

Big Idea 3

The Role of Theories, Laws, Hypotheses, and Models

Naples, Florida

I Wonder Why

South Florida is home to many animals, such as sea turtles. How do scientists help animals survive? *Turn the page to find out.*

Here's Why Scientists in Florida get their hands dirty! They use tools such as tags, cameras, notes, and maps to help animals survive.

Track Your Progress

Essential Questions and Florida Benchmarks

Big Idea 1 *The Practice of Science*

Big Idea 3 *The Role of Theories, Laws, Hypotheses, and Models*

Now I Get the Big Idea!

SC.3.N.1.1 Raise questions about the natural world... **SC.3.N.1.6** Infer based on observation. **SC.3.N.3.1** Recognize that words in science can have different or more specific meanings than their use in everyday language; for example, energy, cell, heat/cold, and evidence. **SC.3.N.3.2** Recognize that scientists use models... **SC.3.N.3.3** Recognize that all models are approximations of natural phenomena...

Essential Question

How Do Scientists Investigate Questions?

Engage Your Brain!

Find the answer to the following question in this lesson and record it here.

How is this student acting like a scientist?

_____

_____

_____

Active Reading

Lesson Vocabulary

List each term. As you learn about each, make notes in the Interactive Glossary.

_____   _____

_____   _____

_____   _____

_____

Use Headings

Active readers preview, or read, the headings first. Headings give the reader an idea of what the reading is about. Reading with a purpose helps active readers understand what they are reading.

What Is Science?

Science is about Earth and everything beyond it. What does a scientist look like? To find out, take a look in the mirror!

Active Reading As you read these two pages, underline the main idea.

Why do volcanoes erupt?

Look for a Question

How does a butterfly use its six legs? What does the shape of a cloud tell about the weather? It's never too soon to start asking questions! Write your own question below.

_____

_____

Science is a way of looking at the world and thinking about it. When you think like a scientist, you ask questions about the world around you. You try to answer your questions by doing investigations.

Some investigations are simple, such as watching animals play. Other investigations take planning. You need to gather and set up materials. Then you write down what happens.

You can think like a scientist on your own or in a group. Sharing what you learn is part of the fun. So get started!

Why does a compass point north?

What do stars look like through a telescope?

What Do You See?

So you want to think like a scientist? Let's get started. Try making some observations and inferences!

Active Reading As you read these two pages, find and underline the definition of *observe*.

Look at the pictures on this page. What do you see? When you use your senses to notice details, you **observe**.

Things you observe can start you thinking. Look at the picture of the small sailboat. You see that it has more than one sail. Now look more closely. The sails are different shapes and sizes.

You might infer that the shape or size of the sails affects how the boat moves. When you **infer**, you offer an explanation of what you observed. You might infer that each sail helps the boat move in a different way.

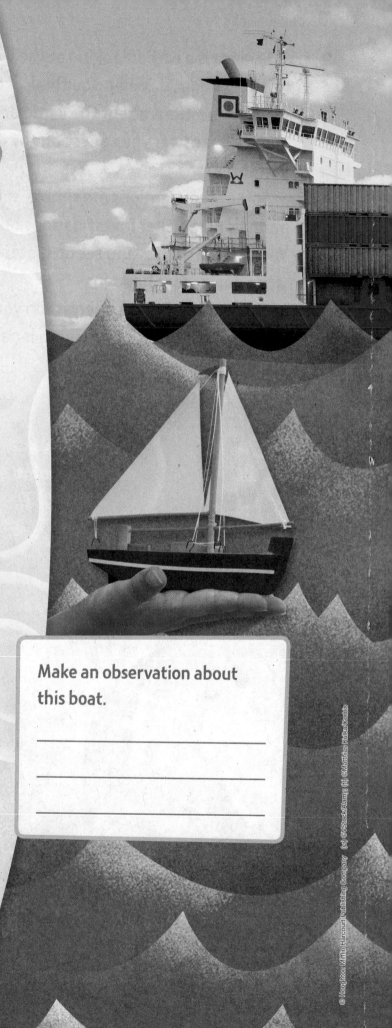

Make an observation about this boat.

_____

_____

_____

Make an observation about this ship.

_____

_____

CONTAINER SHIP

Make an observation about this boat.

_____

_____

623   U.S. COAST GUARD

Write an inference based on this observation:
"I can see the wind blowing this sail."

_____

_____

Getting Answers!

People ask questions all day long. But not all questions are science questions. Science questions can be answered in many ways.

Active Reading As you read these two pages, circle a common, everyday word that has a different meaning in science.

Exploring

Some science questions can be answered by exploring. Say you see a leaf float by on the water. You wonder what else can float on water. You find an eraser in your pocket. You **predict**, or use what you know to tell if it will sink or float. When you know which items float and which don't, you can **classify**, or group, them.

Predict

Think about each item pictured. Then circle the ones you predict will float. Mark an X on those you predict will sink.

Investigating

You might think of an investigation as looking for clues. In science, an **investigation** is a planned way of finding answers to questions. When you do an investigation, you might ask a cause-and-effect question, "Does the amount of weight in a boat affect whether it floats or sinks?" Because you don't want to use a real boat, you can **make and use models.** A raft made of sticks is not exactly like a real boat, but it can be used to learn about them.

Investigating Answers

There are many steps a scientist may take during an investigation. Some do all five described here.

As you read these two pages, number the sentences that describe Onisha's experiment to match the numbered steps in the circles.

1 Ask a Question

What causes things to change? This is the kind of question you can answer with an investigation.

2 Hypothesize

A **hypothesis** is a statement that could answer your question. You must be able to test a hypothesis.

3 Predict and Plan an Investigation

Predict what you will observe if your hypothesis is correct. **Identify the variable** to test, and keep other variables the same.

What Onisha Did …

Onisha thought about rafts floating down a river. She asked a question, "Does the size of a raft affect the amount of weight it can carry?"

Onisha **hypothesizes** that a bigger raft can carry more weight. Then she predicted, "I should be able to add more weight to a bigger raft than to a smaller raft." Onisha planned an investigation called an experiment. Outside of science, experimenting means trying something new, such as a new recipe. In science, an **experiment** is a test done to gather evidence. The evidence might support the hypothesis, or it might not. In her experiment, Onisha built three model rafts that differed only in their number of planks. She carefully put one penny at a time onto each raft until it sank. She recorded her results and drew a conclusion.

Variable

The factor that is changed in an experiment is called a **variable**. It's important to change only one variable at a time.

Draw Conclusions

Analyze your results, and **draw a conclusion.** Ask yourself, "Do the results support my hypothesis?" Share your conclusion with others.

4

Experiment

Now do the experiment to test your hypothesis.

5

▶ What was the variable in Onisha's experiment?

_____

_____

Sum It Up!

When you're done, use the answer key to check and revise your work.

Write words from the lesson that match the pictures.

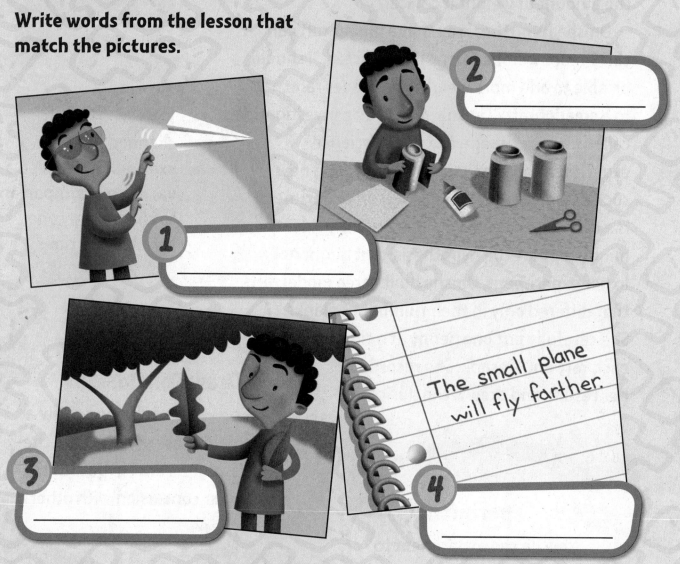

1 _____

2 _____

3 _____

The small plane will fly farther.

4 _____

Use what you learned from the lesson to fill in the sequence below.

observe → **5** _____ → **6** _____ → **7** _____

Brain Check

Name _____

Word Play

1 Use the words in the box to complete the puzzle.

Across

1. You do this when you make a conclusion after observing.

5. the one factor you change in an experiment

6. to make a guess based on what you know or think

8. something that is like the real thing—but not exactly

9. a statement that will answer a question you want to investigate

Down

1. Scientists plan and carry one out to answer their questions.

2. Scientists ask these about the world around them.

3. You do this when you use your five senses.

4. an investigation in which you use variables

7. You draw this at the end of an investigation.

experiment*   infer*   questions   investigation*   variable*   hypothesis*

predict*   model   observe*   conclusion

* Key Lesson Vocabulary

Apply Concepts

2 This bridge is over the Mississippi River. List materials you could use to make a model of it.

_____

_____

3 Greyson wants to know what plants need in order to survive. He places one plant in a window. He places another plant in a dark closet. What is the variable he is testing?

_____

4 Jared looks carefully at a young turtle in his hand. Label each of his statements *observation* or *inference*.

Its front legs are longer than its back legs. _____

It has sharp toenails. _____

It uses its toenails to dig. _____

It can see me. _____

Its shell feels cool and dry against

my hand. _____

Take It Home!

Share what you have learned about observations and inferences with your family. With a family member, make observations and inferences about items in or near your home.

SC.3.N.1.3 Keep records as appropriate, such as pictorial, written, or simple charts and graphs, of investigations conducted. **SC.3.N.1.6** Infer based on observation. **SC.3.N.3.2** Recognize that scientists use models to help understand and explain how things work. **SC.3.N.3.3** Recognize that all models are approximations of natural phenomena; as such, they do not perfectly account for all observations.

Name _____

Essential Question

How Can You Use a Model?

Set a Purpose

What is the question you will try to answer with this investigation?

_____

_____

_____

State Your Hypothesis

Write your hypothesis, or idea you will test.

_____

_____

_____

Think About the Procedure

What is the variable you plan to test?

_____

_____

How will you know whether the variable you changed worked?

_____

_____

Record Your Results

Fill in the chart to record how far the plane flew each time you changed its design.

Change Made to the Model	Distance It Flew

Draw Conclusions

1. Which changes to your model worked best?

_____

_____

_____

_____

2. Was your hypothesis supported by the results? How do you know?

_____

_____

_____

Analyze and Extend

1. How is your model the same as a real airplane?

_____

_____

_____

2. What did you learn about real airplanes from using a model?

_____

_____

_____

3. How is your model different from a real airplane?

_____

_____

_____

_____

_____

4. What can't you learn about real airplanes by using a paper airplane?

_____

_____

_____

_____

5. Think of another question you would like to answer about airplane models.

_____

_____

_____

_____

SC.3.N.1.1 Raise questions about the natural world... **SC.3.N.1.2** Compare the observations made by different groups using the same tools and seek reasons to explain the differences across groups. **SC.3.N.1.3** Keep records as appropriate, such as pictorial, written, or simple charts and graphs...

Essential Question

How Do Scientists Use Tools?

Engage Your Brain!

A hand lens can make a bug look bigger.

What other tools make objects look bigger?

_____

_____

_____

Active Reading

Lesson Vocabulary

List each term. As you learn about each one, make notes in the Interactive Glossary.

_____

_____

_____

Compare and Contrast

Ideas in parts of this lesson explain comparisons and contrasts—they tell how things are alike and different. Active readers focus on comparisons and contrasts when they ask questions such as, How are measuring tools alike and different?

Make It Clear!

Scientists use tools to give them super-vision! Some tools that do this include hand lenses and microscopes.

Active Reading As you read these two pages, circle words or phrases that signal when things are alike and different.

Light microscopes let you see tiny objects by using a light source and lenses or mirrors inside the microscope.

A magnifying box has a lens in its lid.

A hand lens has one lens with a handle.

Use forceps to pick up tiny objects to view with magnifiers.

Use a dropper to move small amounts of liquids for viewing.

Close, Closer, Closest!

Magnifying tools make objects look larger. Hold a hand lens close to one eye. Then move the hand lens closer to the object until it looks large and sharp. A magnifying box is like a hand lens in that it also has one lens. You can put things that are hard to hold, such as a bug, in it.

A **microscope** magnifies objects that are too tiny to be seen with the eye alone. Its power is much greater than that of a hand lens or magnifying box. Most microscopes have two or more lenses that work together.

Pond water as seen with just your eyes.

▶ Draw a picture of how something you see might look if it was magnified.

Pond water as seen through a hand lens.

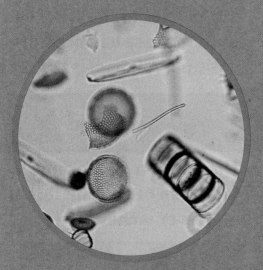

Pond water as seen through a microscope.

Measure It!

Measuring uses numbers to describe the world around you. There are several ways to measure and more than one tool or unit for each way.

Active Reading As you read the next page, circle the main idea.

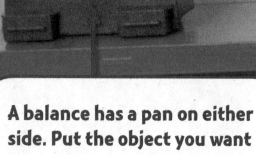

A balance has a pan on either side. Put the object you want to measure on one pan and add masses to the other pan until they are balanced. The basic unit of mass is the gram.

The units on measuring tapes can be centimeters and meters or inches and feet.

ruler

Length, Mass, and Volume

A graduated cylinder has units of volume marked on its side.

Every tool has its purpose! You can **measure** length with rulers and tape measures. Mass is the amount of matter in an object. It is measured with a pan balance. Volume is the amount of space a solid, liquid, or gas takes up.

The volume of a liquid can be measured with a **graduated cylinder** or a measuring cup or spoon. You can also use these tools to find the volume of solids that can be poured, such as sugar or salt. You **use numbers** to report measurements and **compare** objects. You can also **order** things using measurements. You can put pencils in order from shortest to longest.

Measuring cups and spoons are used because the amount of each ingredient is very important.

Do the Math!
Subtract Units

Use a metric ruler to measure the parts of the frog.

1. How many centimeters is the frog's longest front leg?

   _____

2. How many centimeters is the frog's longest back leg?

   _____

3. Now find the difference.

   _____

4. Compare your measurements to those of other students.

   _____

   _____

Time and Temperature

How long did that earthquake shake? Which freezes faster, hot water or cold water? Scientists need tools to answer these questions!

Time

When you count the steady drip of a leaky faucet, you are thinking about time. You can **use time and space relationships.** Clocks and stopwatches are tools that measure time. The base unit of time is the second. One minute is equal to 60 seconds. One hour is equal to 60 minutes.

What if frogs held swim races across a pond? Here two frogs are racing.

START!

Temperature

When you say that ovens are hot or freezers are cold, you are thinking about **temperature**. A thermometer is the tool used to measure temperature. The base units of temperature are called degrees, but all degrees are not the same.

Scientists usually measure temperature in degrees Celsius. Most people around the world use Celsius, too. In the United States, however, degrees Fahrenheit are used to report the weather, body temperature, and in cooking.

▶ The first frog finished the race in 19 seconds. The second frog finished the race in 47 seconds. How much more quickly did the winning frog finish the race?

_____

_____

_____

How Do You Care for Tropical Fish?

To care for tropical fish, you have to think like a scientist and use science tools.

Close Encounters

A public aquarium [uh•KWAIR•ee•uhm] is the place to see sharks and tropical fish. That's where many people get excited about keeping tropical fish at home. The word *aquarium* is used for both the big place you visit and the small tank in your home. Caring for both takes similar skills: observing, inferring, measuring, and recording data.

Does moving your aquarium in front of the window change the water's temperature?

What is the volume of water in your aquarium?

Keep Good Records

Keeping good records is important, whether you're recording data in your science notebook or making entries in your aquarium log. In your log, record the temperature every time you check it. Write the time you feed the fish and the volume of food you give them. Making correct measurements is part of being a good scientist.

Water test kits identify materials in the water.

Taking care of fish means checking the temperature.

Cause and Effect

Every change in an aquarium has a cause. Sometimes fish in an aquarium might become sick. Think of two things that might cause the fish to get sick.

_____

_____

_____

When you're done, use the answer key to
check and revise your work.

**The idea web below summarizes this lesson.
Complete the web.**

How Scientist Use Tools

1 They use hand lenses
and microscopes to make
things look

_____.

They use tools to measure.

2 Length is measured with

_____

_____.

3 A graduated
cylinder measures

_____.

4 Pan balances measure

_____.

5 They measure time
with clocks and

_____.

Brain Check

Name _____

Word Play

1 Write each term after its definition. Then find each term in the word search puzzle.

A. A tool used to measure mass _____

B. A temperature scale used by scientists _____

C. A tool used to pick up tiny objects _____

D. A tool used to measure volume _____

E. A tool you hold against your eye to make objects look bigger _____

F. How hot or cold something is _____

G. A tool that measures temperature _____

H. Something you measure with a stopwatch _____

I. How much space something take up _____

L	T	E	M	P	E	R	A	T	U	R	E	R	M	Y	O	L
U	H	R	P	A	M	I	L	C	E	L	S	I	U	S	V	W
K	E	E	A	V	S	U	N	B	O	W	L	M	A	X	Y	M
N	R	V	N	U	O	M	Z	O	O	L	I	S	S	T	F	O
G	M	C	B	E	U	L	I	H	T	M	A	Y	T	L	O	K
Y	O	Y	A	B	L	U	U	M	I	M	M	Y	O	R	R	J
F	M	S	L	K	K	Z	W	M	M	X	Q	I	P	Z	C	D
K	E	H	A	R	O	O	R	L	E	A	F	S	I	M	E	E
E	T	N	N	R	U	C	L	M	K	P	I	U	T	X	P	H
S	E	N	C	F	I	L	L	H	A	N	D	L	E	N	S	S
J	R	U	E	M	M	U	V	L	V	I	G	T	H	M	I	T
G	R	A	D	U	A	T	E	D	C	Y	L	I	N	D	E	R

Apply Concepts

In 2–5, tell which tool(s) you would use and how you would use them.

 thermometer

measuring spoons

 measuring tape

ruler

magnifying box

2 Find out how long your dog is from nose to tail.

_____
_____
_____

3 Decide if you need to wear a sweatshirt outdoors.

_____
_____
_____

4 Make a bubble bath that has just the right amount of bubbles and is not too hot or too cold.

_____
_____
_____
_____

5 Examine a ladybug and count its legs without hurting it.

_____
_____
_____
_____

© Houghton Mifflin Harcourt Publishing Company   (bl) ©D. Hurst/Alamy

 Take It Home!

Share what you have learned about measuring with your family. With a family member, identify examples of objects you could measure in or near your home.

Name _____

Essential Question

How Can You Measure Length?

SC.3.N.1.1 Raise questions about the natural world... **SC.3.N.1.2** Compare the observations made by different groups...to explain the differences across groups. **SC.3.N.1.3** Keep records as appropriate... **SC.3.N.1.4** Recognize the importance of communication among scientists. **SC.3.N.1.7** Explain that empirical evidence is information, such as observations or measurements, that is used to help validate explanations of natural phenomena.

Set a Purpose

What will you be able to do at the end of this investigation?

_____

_____

_____

Think About the Procedure

What will you think about when choosing the measurement tool for each item?

_____

_____

_____

How will you choose the units that are best for each item?

_____

_____

_____

Record Your Results

In the space below, make a table in which you record your measurements.

Draw Conclusions

1. How does choosing the best tool make measuring length easier?

_____

_____

_____

_____

_____

2. How do units affect the quality of a measurement?

_____

_____

_____

_____

Analyze and Extend

1. Did groups who used the same tools as your group get the same results as you? Explain why or why not.

_____

_____

_____

2. Why was it important to communicate your results with other groups? Explain.

_____

_____

_____

3. When would someone want to use millimeters to find out who throws a ball the farthest? When would using millimeters not be a good choice? (1,000 mm = 1 m)

_____

_____

_____

4. Think of another question you would like to ask about measuring.

_____

_____

_____

Materials

Which tools should you use?

Garter snake

Hemlock tree cone

Ladybug beetle

Bird's feather

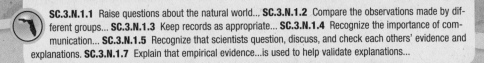

SC.3.N.1.1 Raise questions about the natural world... **SC.3.N.1.2** Compare the observations made by different groups... **SC.3.N.1.3** Keep records as appropriate... **SC.3.N.1.4** Recognize the importance of communication... **SC.3.N.1.5** Recognize that scientists question, discuss, and check each others' evidence and explanations. **SC.3.N.1.7** Explain that empirical evidence...is used to help validate explanations...

Lesson 5

Essential Question

How Do Scientists Record Data?

Engage Your Brain!

People sometimes make statues out of blocks. If you could count how many blocks of each color there are, how would you record this information?

_____

_____

_____

_____

Active Reading

Lesson Vocabulary

List each term. As you learn about each one, make notes in the Interactive Glossary.

_____ _____

_____ _____

Main Ideas

The main idea of a section is the most important idea. The main idea may be stated in the first sentence, or it may be stated elsewhere. Active readers look for main ideas by asking themselves, What is this section mostly about?

Show Me the Evidence

Scientists use observations to answer their questions. You can do this, too!

Active Reading As you read these two pages, find and underline the definitions of *data* and *evidence*.

My data is my *evidence*. It shows that a raft with six planks floats twice as much weight as a raft with only three planks.

Onisha, how do you know that a bigger raft can float more weight than a smaller one?

– I put the pennies on the raft with three planks. It held fewer pennies than the other raft.

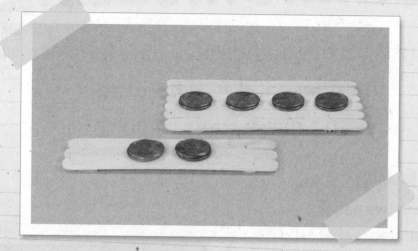

Each science observation is a piece of **data**. For example, the number of pennies on a raft is data.

Onisha finished her investigation and thought about what it meant. She studied her data. Scientists use data as **evidence** to decide whether a hypothesis is or is not supported. Either way, scientists learn valuable things.

Scientists ask other scientists a lot of questions. They compare data. They repeat the investigation to see if they get the same results. Scientists review and talk about the evidence. They agree and disagree while respecting each other's ideas.

Scientists might live too far away to meet face to face. What are three other ways they can share data and discuss evidence?

_____

_____

_____

_____

_____

_____

_____

_____

Communicating Data

Scientists record and display data so others can understand it. There are many ways and many tools to do this.

Active Reading As you read these two pages, circle a sentence that tells the main idea.

How can I communicate my results?

Take a photograph.

You want to find how high different kinds of balls bounce. You test each ball 20 times. How will you record and display your measurements?

_____

_____

After you **gather data,** you can share, or **communicate,** it with others in different ways. How can you **record data?** To show how birds get seeds from a feeder, you can use a camera. To show how a cat cares for her kittens, write it in a journal.

Sometimes scientists use tables and graphs to help **interpret** and **display data.** A **data table** is a display that organizes data into rows and columns. A **bar graph** is used to compare data about different events or groups. Graphs make it easier to see patterns or relationships in data.

Make a bar graph or a data table.

Write in a journal.

You want to record the way the moon seems to change shape for four weeks. What would you use?

_____

_____

You want to describe the kinds of animals you observe living in a stream. Where would you record your observations?

_____

_____

Sum It Up!

Use information in the summary to complete the graphic organizer.

During investigations scientists record their observations, or data. When other scientists ask, "How do you know?", they explain how their data supports their answers. Observations can be shared in many ways. Data in the form of numbers can be shown in data tables and bar graphs. Data can also be shared as diagrams, photos, or in writing.

Main Idea:
Scientists use data to answer questions, and they record it in different ways.

1 Detail: Scientists use their data to answer other scientists' questions.

2 Detail:
_____
_____

3 Detail:
_____
_____

Answer Key: 2. Data can be shown in data tables and bar graphs. 3. Data can also be shared as diagrams, photos, or in writing.

Brain Check

Name _____

Word Play

Find the correct meaning and underline it.

1 Data
- a tool used to measure
- how hot or cold something is
- a piece of science information

2 Evidence
- a kind of graph
- how much space something takes up
- the facts that show if a hypothesis is correct

3 Data table
- a chart for recording numbers
- the number of planks on a raft
- a piece of furniture used by scientists

4 Bar graph
- a chart for recording numbers
- a graph in the shape of a circle
- a graph that shows how things compare

5 Communicate
- take a photograph
- share data with others
- collect and record data

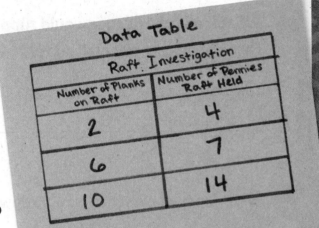

Data Table

Raft Investigation

Number of Planks on Raft	Number of Pennies Raft Held
2	4
6	7
10	14

Bar Graph

Raft Investigation

Apply Concepts

Read the story and answer questions 6–8.

One morning, your dad walks you and your sister to the school bus stop. When you get there, you wonder, "Has the bus come yet?"

6 What kinds of evidence would support the idea that the bus has not arrived yet?

_____

_____

7 What kinds of evidence would show that the bus had already come?

_____

_____

_____

8 Your friend brags that he can throw a baseball 100 meters. What evidence would prove this?

_____

_____

_____

Take It Home!

Share what you have learned about recording evidence with your family. With a family member, identify something you want to observe. Then decide how to record your data.

Name _____

Essential Question

How Do Your Results Compare?

SC.3.N.1.1 Raise questions about the natural world... **SC.3.N.1.2** Compare the observations made by different groups...to explain the differences across groups. **SC.3.N.1.3** Keep records as appropriate... **SC.3.N.1.4** Recognize the importance of communication among scientists. **SC.3.N.1.5** Recognize that scientists question, discuss, and check each others' evidence and explanations. **SC.3.N.1.7** Explain that empirical evidence is information...used to help validate explanations of natural phenomena.

Set a Purpose

What will you learn from this investigation?

_____

_____

State Your Hypothesis

Tell how you think the height of bubbles in water relates to the amount of dishwashing liquid used.

_____

_____

_____

Think About the Procedure

List the things you did that were the same each time.

_____

_____

_____

Describe the variable, the one thing you changed each time.

_____

_____

_____

Record Data

In the space below, make a table to record your measurements.

Draw Conclusions

Look back at your hypothesis. Did your results support it? Explain your answer.

_____

_____

_____

Analyze and Extend

1. Why is it helpful to compare results with others?

_____

_____

_____

2. What would you do if you found out that your results were very different from those of others?

_____

_____

_____

3. The bar graph below shows the height of the column of bubbles produced by equal amounts of three brands of dishwashing liquid. What does this data show?

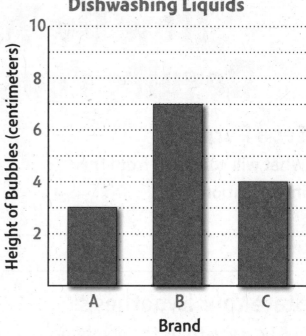

Bubbles Made by Dishwashing Liquids

_____

_____

_____

4. Think of other questions you would like to ask about bubbles.

_____

_____

_____

1

A meteorologist is a person who studies weather.

2

Meteorologists use tools to measure temperature, wind speed, and air pressure.

3

Meteorologists use data they collect to forecast the weather.

6
THINGS
You Should Know About
Meteorologists

4

Computers help meteorologists share weather data from around the world.

5

Keeping good records helps meteorologists see weather patterns.

6

Meteorologists' forecasts help people stay safe during bad weather.

Be a Meteorologist

Answer the questions below using the Weather Forecast bar graph.

1 What was the temperature on Thursday? _____

2 Which day was cloudy and rainy? _____

3 How much cooler was it on Tuesday than Thursday?

_____

4 Which day was partly cloudy? _____

5 Compare the temperatures on Tuesday and Friday. Which day had the higher temperature?

_____

6 In the forecast below, which day has the highest temperature _____? The lowest?

_____

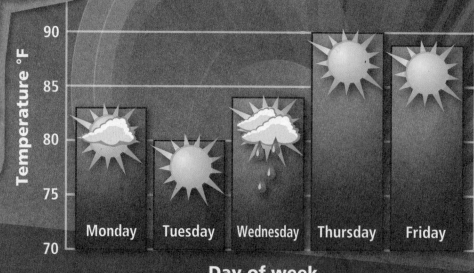

WEATHER FORECAST

Temperature °F

90
85
80
75
70

Monday   Tuesday   Wednesday   Thursday   Friday

Day of week

Multiple Choice

Identify the choice that best answers the question.

SC.3.N.1.4, SC.3.N.1.5

1 Jamie does an electricity experiment for homework. She must communicate the results. Which of these ideas is a way to communicate results?

(A) ask herself questions

(B) develop a conclusion

(C) form a hypothesis

(D) write a report

SC.3.N.1.1

2 A class is doing an experiment. The students want to know if tadpoles' health depends on the water they live in. They put the tadpoles into three tanks.

Tank	Type of water	Activity
A	clean tap water	Students will use treatments to keep the water clean.
B	clean tap water	Students will begin with clean water, but will not keep it clean.
C	clean tap water plus lots of dirt	Students will add a tablespoon of dirt every other day.

Which variable is being tested?

(F) number of tanks

(G) size of the tadpoles

(H) amount of dirt in the water

(I) amount of water in the tanks

SC.3.N.1.1

3 Misha wants to find out if air takes up space. Which experiment would **best** help her find this out?

(A) Weigh an empty metal container. Place a lid on it. Weigh it again.

(B) Blow up a balloon. Tie a knot to make sure it is closed. Try to flatten it.

(C) Take a cup and fill it with water. Fill another cup with air. Weigh them.

(D) Put red food coloring in an empty bottle, and see if the air turns red.

SC.3.N.1.6

4 Some shells have two parts. The animal can open the parts or close them tightly. The shell part in the picture is one that Yoshiko found.

Which could be the other part of the shell Yoshiko found?

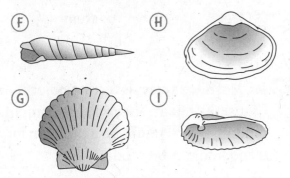

(F)   (H)

(G)   (I)

SC.3.N.1.2

5 The Orasco family wants to put a fence around their house. Which of these is the **best** estimate for how much fencing the Orasco family will need?

(A) 20 mm   (C) 2 m

(B) 20 cm   (D) 200 m

SC.3.N.3.1

6 Kisha counts the number of brown dogs she sees at a park. Would a scientist say that Kisha did an experiment?

- (F) Yes, because she only counted dogs.
- (G) Yes, because she was at the park.
- (H) No, because she did not do a test to gather evidence.
- (I) No, because dogs cannot be used in experiments.

SC.3.N.3.2

7 Soon-Yi is using a model to investigate the parts of a plant in class. She cannot identify the part marked with an X.

Use the illustration to identify the part marked with an X.

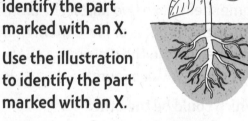

- (A) bud
- (B) leaf
- (C) root
- (D) stem

SC.3.N.3.3

8 Mr. Martinez's class is testing objects that sink or float. They will use computer models. Which might be a problem in using a computer model?

- (F) Not everyone will get to take a turn.
- (G) The class may not have a computer.
- (H) You can test only what is in the computer program.
- (I) You can test materials that are not in your classroom.

SC.3.N.1.7

9 Kia wants to know what types of trees grow the fastest. She looks at this table and sees she needs more information.

Age of tree (yr)	Height (m)
1	2
5	3
10	4
20	6

What information does she need?

- (A) the height of each tree
- (B) the age of each tree in months
- (C) each type of tree that was measured
- (D) the date the trees were measured

SC.3.N.1.4, SC.3.N.1.5

10 Omid did an experiment with radishes. He concluded that radishes grow best in full sunlight. He presents his experiment at a science fair. Why should Omid include his data with his presentation?

- (F) The judges would have data to read.
- (G) The judges would know he grew the plants.
- (H) The judges would want to learn more about the topic.
- (I) The judges could see if his data supported his conclusion.

SC.3.N.1.6

11 Greyson observes a nest in a tree. What might Greyson infer about the nest?

- (A) The nest was made by a lizard.
- (B) The nest was made by a bird.
- (C) The nest does not have eggs in it.
- (D) The nest is made of grass.

SC.3.N.1.1, SC.3.N.1.7

12 Eduardo fills six jars each with 400 mL of water. He places three of them outside in sunny spots. He places the other three outside in shady spots. He waits 4 hours. Then he measures how much water is left in each jar. He graphs the data.

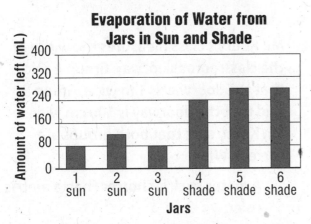

Evaporation of Water from Jars in Sun and Shade

Which conclusion is supported?

(F) Water gets hotter in the shade than in the sun.

(G) Water gets hotter in the sun than in the shade.

(H) Water evaporates more quickly in the shade than in the sun.

(I) Water evaporates more quickly in the sun than in the shade.

SC.3.N.1.3

13 Ilse did an experiment to determine the height of bubbles that would form in jars with different amounts of soap. How should he display his results?

(A) take a photo

(B) draw a bar graph

(C) draw the bubbles

(D) write it in a paragraph

SC.3.N.1.7

14 The bar graph below shows the number of students who have different types of pets.

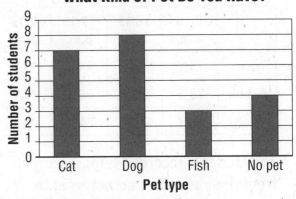

What Kind of Pet Do You Have?

Which statement is **best** supported by the data from the survey?

(F) Some students do not have pets.

(G) Most people do not like cats or dogs.

(H) Most people like dogs more than they like cats.

(I) Fish are easier to take care of than dogs or cats.

SC.3.N.1.3

15 Mrs. Harris's class is doing an experiment to see if cut flowers stay fresh longer in warm water or in cold water. Mrs. Harris created the table below.

	Roses	Daisies	Mums
Warm water			
Cold water			

What should students write in the different rows of the table?

(A) the length of each stem

(B) the size of each flower

(C) the number of petals on each flower

(D) the date each flower wilts

SC.3.N.1.2

16 Three students observed the outside air temperature throughout the day. Their findings are below.

	8:15 a.m.	10:15 a.m.	12:15 p.m.	2:15 p.m.
Lucia	75 °F	78 °F	84 °F	89 °F
Ashok	75 °F	78 °F	85 °F	88 °F
Emily	75 °F	77 °F	84 °F	88 °F

The students recorded temperatures from their own thermometers in the same area each time. What could be a reason for the slight differences in the temperatures they recorded?

(F) The students could not read the thermometers.

(G) The students looked at the thermometers at different times.

(H) One of the thermometers was broken so its readings were different.

(I) Some of the readings were in between the marks so the students decided which mark was closest.

SC.3.N.3.1

17 Why is it important to use scientific terms to describe clouds that you observe?

(A) All clouds look the same.

(B) Different cloud types are likely to appear at different times.

(C) If you describe a cloud as an animal, people will not believe you.

(D) People may have different ideas of "fluffy" or "thin," but the scientific terms are clearly defined.

SC.3.N.1.2

18 Which item would be **easier** to measure using a 25-ft tape measure than using a 12-in. ruler?

(F) beetle

(G) book

(H) classroom

(I) postage stamp

SC.3.N.1.2

19 Mr. Koury's class measures the width of the classroom's doorway. Group A said that the doorway is 1 m wide. Group B said that the doorway is 100 cm wide. Mr. Koury says that both groups are correct. Why?

(A) A meter stick is shorter than a metric ruler.

(B) The metric ruler is more accurate than the meter stick.

(C) The groups' measurements, 1 m and 100 cm, are the same length.

(D) When you use two different tools to measure the same object, you should get two very different answers.

SC.3.N.1.1

20 A class measures the outside air temperature at the same time each day for a month, and then compares the findings. Which tells the **most** detailed information about the experiment?

(F) Many days were warm.

(G) The coldest day was 5 °C.

(H) It rained on several of the days.

(I) Some days were cooler than others.

UNIT 2
Earth and Stars

Big Idea 5

Earth in Space and Time

Big Idea 6

Earth Structures

Florida as seen from space.

I Wonder Why

Astronauts in space can see views of Earth like this. Why are astronauts able to travel into space? *Turn the page to find out.*

Here's Why Astronauts are sent into space in space vehicles. They are still affected by Earth's gravity.

Track Your Progress

Essential Questions and Florida Benchmarks

Big Idea 5 *Earth in Space and Time*

Big Idea 6 *Earth Structures*

Now I Get the Big Idea!

.5.1 Explain that stars can be different... **SC.3.E.5.2** Identify the Sun as a star that emits energy;
of it in the form of light. **SC.3.E.5.3** Recognize that the Sun appears large and bright because it is the
t star to Earth. **SC.3.E.5.5** Investigate that the number of stars that can be seen through telescopes is
y greater... **SC.3.E.6.1** Demonstrate that radiant energy from the Sun can heat objects...

Lesson **1**

ential Question

What Are the Sun and Stars?

Engage Your Brain!

Find the answer to the following question in this lesson and record it here.

How can a star affect Earth?

_____

_____

_____

Active Reading

esson Vocabulary

t the terms. As you learn about
ch one, make notes in the Interactive
ossary.

_____

_____

Using Headings

Active readers preview headings and use them to pose questions about the material they will read. Reading to find an answer helps active readers focus on understanding and remembering what they read.

Stars
Up Close!

On a clear night you can see many stars in the sky. By day, you see the sun shining. How are the sun and other stars alike and different?

Active Reading As you read these two pages, underline the definition of *sun*.

The Sun

Our **sun** is a medium-size star. The sun appears much larger than other stars. It also appears much brighter. That is because the sun is much closer to Earth than other stars are.

From Earth, our sun looks like a giant ball of light. The sun, like other stars, gives off light and heat.

The way the sun looks close up is very different from the way it looks from Earth.

Stars

A **star** is a ball of hot, glowing gases. From Earth most stars look like small points of light. This is because they are far away. The sun and other stars are both present in the daytime. You cannot see the other stars because the sun makes the sky so bright.

The surface of other stars may look very much like the surface of our sun.

▶ **Compare and contrast** the sun with one of the stars shown on this page. Tell two ways they are alike and two ways they are different.

Sun	Both Stars	Other Star

Great Balls of Fire

From far away, stars look very similar. Up close, stars have many different characteristics. How are stars alike? How are they different?

Active Reading Draw circles around the headings. What are you going to read about stars? Read to see if you were correct.

▶ Use the space below to draw your own star. Describe your star based upon its color, size, and brightness.

Stars are born in giant clouds of gas and dust like this one.

Brightness

Brightness tells how much light a star gives off. A very bright star gives off a lot of light. Some stars are much brighter than our sun. Others are dimmer.

Size

Supergiant stars are the largest stars. Hundreds or thousands of our sun could fit inside one supergiant star! The smallest stars are called white dwarfs. Space is filled with many different kinds of beautiful stars!

Color

Stars have different colors. Our sun is a yellow star. Blue, white, and red are other colors of stars. Blue stars are the hottest. Red stars are the coolest.

Full of Energy

Earth would be a cold, dark, and empty planet without the sun. Life could not survive. Read on to find out why.

The Sun Lights Earth

Radiant [RAY•dee•uhnt] energy is energy that can travel through space! Stars give off radiant energy. The sun is our closest star. Some of its radiant energy travels to Earth as light. This light energy helps people and animals see.

Plants use light energy to make their own food. Without light energy from the sun, there could be no plants on Earth. So without the sun, there would be no plants or animals on Earth.

The sun's light makes day brighter than night.

The Sun Heats Earth

Other radiant energy from the sun warms Earth's land, air, and water. During the night, some heat leaves Earth. That is why it is cooler at night than during the day.

You cannot see the sun's energy heating Earth, but you can feel it. When you walk on a beach heated by the sun, the sand feels hot. Without the sun's radiant energy, Earth would be too cold for people to live.

Plants need light to survive.

▶ Draw a picture to show how the sun affects something on Earth.

The sun's energy warms Earth's water.

Stargazing

Away from city lights, you can see thousands of stars in the night sky. You can see many more stars if you use a telescope.

A **telescope** is a tool that makes faraway objects seem larger. It makes faraway objects seem closer, too. With a telescope, you can see many more stars than you can with your eyes. Stars that are bright look even brighter. Stars that are dim look brighter, too.

Even with a telescope, most stars look like points of light in the sky. That's because they are so far away. Only the sun looks different. The sun is much closer to Earth than the other stars. Because the sun is so close to Earth, you should never look directly at it.

A telescope is a long tube with lenses at both ends. The lenses make objects appear larger and closer.

© Houghton Mifflin Harcourt Publishing Company (bkgd) ©Larry Landolt/Photo Researchers, Inc; (inset) ©Creatas/Age Fotostock

58

With a telescope, stars look brighter and clearer.

You can see many stars with just your eyes.

Do the Math!
Solve a Word Problem

Max looks at a part of the sky through a hollow tube. He counts 8 stars. Then he looks at the sky with a telescope. He sees 5 times as many stars. How many stars does Max see now?

_____

Sum It Up!

When you're done, use the answer key to check and revise your work.

Read the summary statements below. Each one is incorrect.
Change the circled part of the summary to make it correct.

1 The sun is a star that gives off light and (electric energy).
_____

2 Stars look like (flashes) of light in the night sky.
_____

3 You can see (fewer) stars with a telescope than with just your eyes.
_____

4 The sun is a ball of hot, glowing (clouds.)
_____

5 Stars are grouped by their color, brightness, and (shape.)
_____

Answer Key: 1. heat 2. points 3. more 4. gases 5. size

Brain Check

Name _____

Word Play

1 Read each definition below. Write the word. Then find and circle the word in the Word Search.

A ball of hot, glowing gases _____

The kind of energy from the sun that helps people see _____

An instrument that makes stars look brighter and closer _____

The star that is closest to Earth _____

The kind of energy that can move through space _____

Features of stars are brightness, size, and _____

b	v	t	e	r	d	s	a	p	i	u	l	w	m	o	q	j
a	b	t	h	y	j	d	f	w	e	x	s	o	l	k	m	g
r	y	c	t	e	l	e	s	c	o	p	e	u	a	h	s	d
v	c	b	n	r	t	i	a	e	k	i	l	o	s	e	d	b
p	o	e	w	g	t	x	g	p	o	s	t	y	p	a	h	k
x	l	e	r	i	d	t	a	h	u	b	g	s	s	t	a	r
w	o	a	g	t	d	r	a	p	t	h	m	u	a	d	o	n
i	r	a	d	i	a	n	t	p	q	y	d	n	d	f	w	b
y	d	r	l	o	g	a	r	m	b	r	t	d	a	c	z	y

Apply Concepts

2 Draw stars you might see with your eyes. Then draw stars you might see with a telescope.

Your Eyes

A Telescope

3 Think about the characteristics of stars. Draw one. Describe its color, size, and brightness.

_____

_____

4 The sun shines on the town in the picture. Tell some of the ways that the sun affects this town.

_____

_____

_____

Take It Home! Share what you have learned about the sun with your family. With a family member, identify three ways the sun affects your everyday life.

Name _____

SC.3.N.3.2 Recognize that scientists use models... SC.3.N.3.3 Recognize that all models are approximations... SC.3.E.5.1 Explain that stars can be different; some are smaller, some are larger, and some appear brighter than others; all except the Sun are so far away that they look like points of light. SC.3.E.5.5 Investigate that the number of stars that can be seen through telescopes is dramatically greater than those seen by the unaided eye.

Essential Question

How Many Stars Do You See?

Set a Purpose

What do you think you will learn from observing the box with pinholes?

_____

_____

_____

_____

Think About the Procedure

Why do you think you are observing the points of light from different distances?

_____

_____

_____

Record Your Data

In the space below, make a data table to record what you observe. Compare your data with data collected by your classmates.

Draw Conclusions

How were the points of light you observed different from far away, from close up, and through the hand lens?

_____

_____

_____

_____

_____

_____

Analyze and Extend

1. Did you count more points of light from far away or from close up?

_____

_____

_____

2. Infer what you would see if you moved even closer to the box.

_____

_____

_____

_____

3. In the box below, draw what a point of light looked like from a distance. Then draw what it looked like when it was closer.

_____

4. For what tool is the hand lens a model? How is the model like that tool?

_____

_____

_____

_____

_____

64

SC.3.N.1.5 Recognize that scientists question, discuss, and check each others' evidence and explanations.
SC.3.E.6.1 Demonstrate that radiant energy from the Sun can heat objects and when the Sun is not present, heat may be lost.

Name _____

Essential Question

How Does the Sun Heat Earth?

Set a Purpose

What will you learn from this activity?

_____

_____

_____

Think About the Procedure

Why do you think some students moved their cup from the sunny spot into the shade?

_____

_____

_____

Record Your Data

Use your Science Notebook. Record the temperatures in a data table. Use it to make a bar graph here.

Temperature (°C)

Time (hours)

Draw Conclusions

How did the heat from the sun affect the soil in the cups?

_____

_____

_____

Analyze and Extend

1. Share the data in your bar graphs. Which thermometer showed the greatest increase in temperature? How do you know?

_____

_____

_____

_____

2. What happened to the thermometer that was moved into the shade? Why do you think this happened?

_____

_____

_____

_____

3. In the box below, draw a way that radiant energy from the sun affects organisms on Earth.

4. How did the bar graphs help you communicate your data?

_____

_____

_____

_____

5. What other question would you like to ask about how the sun heats Earth?

_____

_____

_____

SC.3.N.1.5 Recognize that scientists question, discuss, and check each others' evidence and explanations. **SC.3.E.5.1** Explain that stars can be different; some are smaller, some are larger, and some appear brighter than others; all except the Sun are so far away that they look like points of light.

People in Science

Meet the Stargazers

Ellen Ochoa
1958–

In school, Ellen Ochoa loved math and science. Ochoa worked hard in school and became a scientist. She invented optical equipment that can help explore objects in space. She used a robotic arm to work with machines in space. In 1991, Ochoa was the first Hispanic woman to become an astronaut.

On a space flight, Ochoa used a robotic arm to capture an orbiting telescope.

Subrahmanyan
Chandrasekhar
1910–1995

Subrahmanyan Chandrasekhar studied how stars change. He discovered that stars can be many different sizes. Some stars slowly become cool. Others collapse into a black hole. Scientists questioned his discovery, but years later accepted it. In 1983, Chandrasekhar won the Nobel Prize for his work with stars.

The collapse of a star can form a black hole. In a black hole, light cannot escape.

Crossword Puzzle

| astronaut | optical | black hole | size | Ochoa | Prize |

Read each clue and write the answer in the correct squares.

Across

1. where light cannot escape
3. Chandrasekhar was awarded the Nobel _____.
4. a person trained to work in space

Down

2. Ochoa invented _____ equipment.
5. Stars can be different in _____.
6. first Hispanic woman astronaut

© Houghton Mifflin Harcourt Publishing Company

SC.3.E.5.4 Explore the Law of Gravity by demonstrating that gravity is a force that can be overcome.

Lesson 4

Essential Question

What Is Gravity?

Engage Your Brain!

Find the answer to the following question in this lesson and record it here.

Why are these skydivers falling toward Earth?

_____

_____

_____

Active Reading

Lesson Vocabulary

List the terms. As you learn about each one, make notes in the Interactive Glossary.

_____

_____

Cause and Effect

Some ideas in this lesson are connected by a cause-and-effect relationship. What makes something happen is a cause. What happens because of something else is an effect. Active readers look for effects by asking themselves, What happened? They look for causes by asking, Why did it happen?

Gravity!

If you let go of a basketball, it will not stay in the air. It falls to the ground. What makes it fall?

As you read this page, draw one line under a cause. Draw two lines under an effect.

Objects fall because a force pulls them to the ground. A **force** is a push or a pull. The force that causes objects to fall is called gravity. **Gravity** is a force that pulls objects toward one another. It pulls objects toward Earth. If you jump into the air, gravity will pull you back to Earth. Because of gravity's pull, the planets travel in paths around the sun.

What goes up, must come down. That's because of gravity!

▶ Draw some examples of gravity at work that you have seen today.

You may not think about it, but you see how gravity works every day. These photos show gravity at work.

The penguin in the top photo is diving off a cliff. It doesn't hang in the air, and it doesn't float up! Gravity pulls the penguin down toward Earth and into the water.

In the bottom photo, kids are going down a slide. Gravity pulls them toward Earth. The slide keeps them from falling straight down.

Gravity helps this penguin quickly get into the water.

These kids are using gravity to have some fun!

Stop it!

The kids on the previous page do not fall straight down. Instead, they slide safely to the ground. The slide changes the effect of gravity on their motion.

Active Reading As you read these two pages, circle examples of objects that can overcome gravity.

You know that gravity is a force. Other forces can *oppose*, or act against, gravity. Picture a baseball player catching a fly ball in his mitt. The mitt stops the ball from falling to the ground. Gravity has been opposed.

When you catch a falling ball, you balance gravity's pull.

The force of this rocket opposes gravity. The force is strong enough for the rocket to leave the ground.

This skywalk hangs over the Grand Canyon. It pushes up on people's feet. The force is strong enough to keep people from falling into the canyon below.

The air pushes up on this hang glider. The push of the air opposes the pull of gravity.

The pictures on these pages show more ways that gravity can be opposed. Look at the hang glider. Air pushes up on the glider. Because this upward force opposes gravity, the hang glider does not fall to Earth. The rocket in the picture on the previous page works against Earth's gravity. The rocket goes up into the sky. It takes a force greater than the force of Earth's gravity to launch the rocket.

Keep It Up!

What are some ways you can overcome gravity? Make a list.

_____

_____

_____

_____

Sum It Up! →

When you're done, use the answer key to check and revise your work.

Complete the summary. Use the information to complete the graphic organizer.

A push or pull is a (1) _____. Gravity is a kind of force. It pulls objects toward each other. Gravity is what holds objects on

(2) _____. Sometimes people

can overcome (3) _____. For example, a person can catch a ball in the air. A rocket can be launched. A person can soar in a hang glider.

Summarize

Main Idea: Gravity is a force that pulls objects toward Earth, but other forces can oppose gravity.

Detail: (4)	**Detail: (5)**	**Detail:** Gravity enables a bird to dive.
_____	_____	
_____	_____	
_____	_____	
_____	_____	
_____	_____	

74

Answer Key: 1. force 2. Earth 3. gravity 4. Sample answer: Gravity is the reason people fall down. 5. Sample answer: A rocket can oppose gravity.

© Houghton Mifflin Harcourt Publishing Company   (t) ©Getty Images; (b) ©Arthur Morris/Corbis

Name _____

Word Play

Look at the picture clues. Fill in the correct term. Circle the letters with numbers underneath them.

1

The ball is pulled by

__ __ __ __ __ __
    8   6

2

A push or a pull

__ __ __ __ __
   5   1

3

A kind of force

__ __ __ __ __
3 2

4

Gravity is

__ __ __ __ __ __ __ __ __
                4   7

5 Look at the letters in circles. Match the letter with the number below each space. Then solve the riddle.

What is an astronaut's favorite drink?

A __ __ __ __ __ G R A V I - __ __ __
   1 2 3   4 5   6 7 8

Apply Concepts

Is gravity being opposed? Write *yes* or *no*.

_____   _____   _____

9 Look at the picture below. Describe how the rocket opposes the force of gravity.

_____

_____

_____

_____

_____

_____

_____

Take It Home!

With your family, take a short walk outdoors. Identify two objects that are affected by gravity. For each thing, discuss how gravity affects both that object and you.

Multiple Choice

Identify the choice that best answers the question.

SC.3.E.5.4

1 What is a force?

Ⓐ a living thing

Ⓑ a push or a pull

Ⓒ a kind of energy

Ⓓ a type of chemical

SC.3.E.6.1, SC.3.N.1.1

2 A weather forecaster measures the air temperature in Tampa. The graph shows her data from 9:00 p.m. to 5:00 a.m.

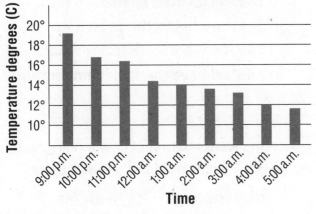

Tampa, FL Overnight Temperatures March 10–March 11

Which **best** explains the data?

Ⓕ The air cools down after 9 p.m.

Ⓖ The air warms up after 9 p.m.

Ⓗ The temperature does not change.

Ⓘ The air gets warmer before sunrise.

SC.3.E.6.1

3 Marta had a picnic. She placed one bag of ice on a table in the shade and another bag in the sun. Both bags were the same size and shape. The ice placed in the sun melted more quickly. Why?

Ⓐ The bags of ice were different types.

Ⓑ A summer day is usually warmer than a winter day.

Ⓒ One table was larger than the other.

Ⓓ Things heat up more quickly in the sun than in the shade.

SC.3.E.6.1, SC.3.N.1.2

4 Two students want to sit outside in a place that is the coolest from 11:00 a.m. to 1:00 p.m. One thinks a shady spot will be cooler, but the other thinks a sunny spot would be just as cool. How could they use two thermometers to find out?

Ⓕ Compare the temperatures of the shady spot and a classroom from 11:00 a.m. to 1:00 p.m.

Ⓖ Compare the temperatures of the sunny spot and a classroom from 11:00 a.m. to 1:00 p.m.

Ⓗ Compare the temperatures of the shady spot and the sunny spot from 11:00 a.m. to 1:00 p.m.

Ⓘ Compare the temperature of the shady spot from 11:00 a.m. to 1:00 p.m. with its temperature from 9:00 a.m. to 11:00 a.m.

SC.3.E.5.2, SC.3.N.1.5

5 Tommy and Maura record how many hours of sunlight they received on the first day of summer. Tommy lives in Alaska. Maura lives in Florida. How could they double-check their own data?

Ⓐ Record the hours again on the first day of winter.

Ⓑ Record the hours again from their own homes.

Ⓒ Go to each other's house and record the hours again.

Ⓓ Go to Texas and record the hours of sunlight together.

SC.3.E.6.1

6 An astronaut in space can see planets, moons, stars, and Earth in the sky. Which **most likely** makes its own light?

Ⓕ star   Ⓗ moon

Ⓖ Earth   Ⓘ planet

SC.3.E.5.2

7 Joel knows the sun's radiant energy travels through space to Earth. Which is **not** an effect of radiant energy on Earth?

Ⓐ It causes Earth's land to heat up.

Ⓑ It causes Earth's oceans to heat up.

Ⓒ It causes objects to fall to Earth.

Ⓓ It lights up the daytime sky.

SC.3.E.5.5

8 Liam wants to observe stars in the night sky. Which tool would be **most** helpful?

Ⓕ

Ⓗ

Ⓖ

Ⓘ

SC.3.E.5.1

9 One way scientists classify stars is by color. Blue stars are the hottest. Red stars are the coolest. The sun is a yellow star. Which statement is true?

Ⓐ The sun is cooler than a red star.

Ⓑ The sun is hotter than a blue star.

Ⓒ The sun is hotter than a red star.

Ⓓ All stars have the same temperature.

SC.3.E.5.5, SC.3.N.3.2

10 Keisha wants to model how a telescope works. Which could she use as a model?

Ⓕ microscope   Ⓗ hand lens

Ⓖ telescope   Ⓘ goggles

SC.3.E.5.1, SC.3.N.1.3

11 A class uses a black box with pinholes and a lamp to model a night sky. They will count the stars from two distances. Which observation gives the **most** details about the stars?

Ⓐ I saw the same number of stars both times I looked.

Ⓑ I counted 6 large, 11 medium, and 7 small stars on the box.

Ⓒ I saw stars in patterns of circles, squares, and rectangles.

Ⓓ I counted by making marks on a separate piece of paper for each star.

SC.3.E.5.1, SC.3.E.5.3

12 Hannah notices that the stars and the sun appear very different. Which statement **best** tells why other stars appear different from the sun?

Ⓕ The stars are not as hot as the sun.

Ⓖ The stars are smaller than the sun.

Ⓗ The stars are closer to Earth.

Ⓘ The stars are farther from Earth.

SC.3.E.5.4

13 Which is an example of overcoming gravity?

Ⓐ jumping in a pool

Ⓑ dropping a ball

Ⓒ skiing down a hill

Ⓓ catching a baseball

SC.3.E.5.4

14 Grant jumps into the air. Why does he come back down?

Ⓕ He did not jump on a trampoline.

Ⓖ He did not jump with tennis shoes on.

Ⓗ There is not enough air between his feet and the ground.

Ⓘ There is no force that overcomes gravity's force on him.

SC.3.E.5.1

15 This picture shows stars in a night sky.

What information can you discover by looking at the picture?

Ⓐ Brighter stars are closest to Earth.

Ⓑ The smallest stars are the brightest.

Ⓒ The largest stars are part of the sun.

Ⓓ Stars look different from one another.

SC.3.E.5.4

16 Imagine that there was suddenly no gravity on Earth. What would **most likely** happen to a picture hanging on a nail?

(F) The picture would fall to the floor.

(G) The picture would float off the nail.

(H) The picture would shoot upward.

(I) You would not be able to get the picture off the nail.

SC.3.E.5.5, SC.3.N.3.3

17 Marisa uses a black box with pinholes of different sizes to model the night sky. In what way is the box **not** a good model for the night sky?

(A) Marisa's model shows that stars give off light.

(B) Marisa's model shows the stars as having different sizes.

(C) Marisa's model only shows stars in the night sky.

(D) Marisa's model shows that stars appear as points of light in the sky.

SC.3.E.5.3, SC.3.N.3.2

18 Ally wants to use a model to show her class that the sun appears larger than other stars because it is closer to Earth. What could she use as her model?

(F) a drawing of a large star and the sun

(G) two foam balls of the same size

(H) a picture of the sun next to a picture of a star

(I) a model of the sun, Earth, and other planets

SC.3.E.5.2, SC.3.N.1.5

19 Angie does a test to see if plants need light from the sun to grow. After her test, she says that plants do not need light to grow. Marco questions her results. How could he check her evidence?

(A) Ask Angie to show her data.

(B) Repeat Angie's test.

(C) Discuss Angie's results with others.

(D) Watch plants grow in a park.

SC.3.E.5.4

20 The dotted line in the figure shows the path of a thrown stick.

Why does the path curve?

(F) Gravity is pulling the stick down.

(G) The dog is pulling the stick down.

(H) The person used a curve-ball throw.

(I) The air pushes down on the stick.

Properties of Matter

Big Idea 8

Properties of Matter

Big Idea 9

Changes in Matter

Coral Reef in
Key Largo, Florida

I Wonder Why

The colors of coral and fish can help us
learn how to use properties of matter.
Why is this so? *Turn the page to find out.*

Here's Why Color is a physical property of matter. You can use color to sort coral and fish into groups.

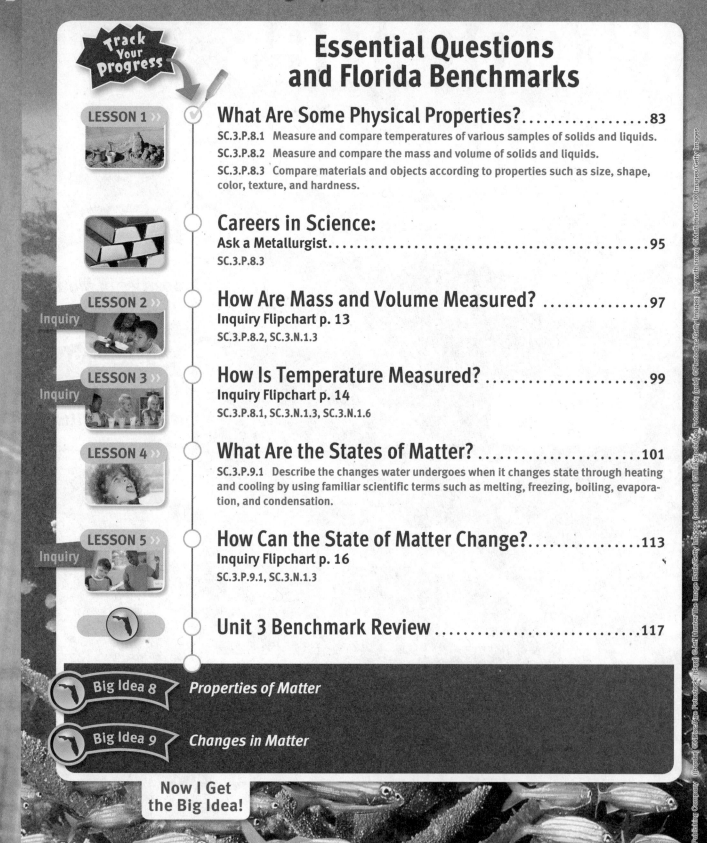

Track Your Progress

Essential Questions and Florida Benchmarks

Big Idea 8 *Properties of Matter*

Big Idea 9 *Changes in Matter*

Now I Get the Big Idea!

SC.3.P.8.1 Measure and compare temperatures of various samples of solids and liquids. **SC.3.P.8.2** Measure and compare the mass and volume of solids and liquids.
SC.3.P.8.3 Compare materials and objects according to properties such as size, shape, color, texture, and hardness.

Essential Question

What Are Some Physical Properties?

Engage Your Brain!

Find the answer to the question in this lesson and record it here.

How can you compare these beach umbrellas?

_____

_____

_____

Active Reading

Lesson Vocabulary

List the terms, and make notes in the Interactive Glossary as you learn more.

_____

_____

_____

_____

Compare and Contrast

Many ideas in this lesson are connected because they explain comparisons and contrasts—how things are alike and different. Active readers stay focused on comparisons and contrasts when they ask themselves, How are things alike? How are they different?

It's Everything!

What is matter? Everything you see on this page is matter. All the "stuff" around you is matter.

Active Reading As you read the next page, draw a line under each main idea.

Texture is the way something feels. Objects can be smooth or rough. What is the texture of sand?

_____

_____

Matter can be different colors. Write a sentence that describes the color of the beach ball.

_____

_____

Matter is anything that takes up space. Your science book takes up more space than your pencil does. Did you know that no two things can take up the same space?

You describe matter by naming its physical properties. A **physical property** is a characteristic of matter that you can observe or measure directly. Look in the boxes to learn about some properties of matter.

Even we are made of matter!

Hardness describes how easily an object's shape can be changed. Name a hard object you see.

_____

_____

_____

_____

Size is how big something is. Which object is the biggest? Which one takes up the most space?

_____

_____

Shape is the form an object has. What words can you use to describe the two smallest shells?

_____

_____

_____

How Much Mass?

Why is it so difficult to lift a bucket full of water? Would it be easier to carry the water in smaller containers instead?

Active Reading As you read these two pages, find and underline the definition of *mass*. Then circle the name of the tool we use to measure mass.

Mass is the amount of matter an object has. Mass is also a measure of how hard it is to move an object. The more mass an object has, the harder it is to move the object.

How can you measure the mass of sand, water, or other materials in a bucket? Check out the next page.

We use a pan balance to measure mass. The pan balance measures mass in grams (g). How can you measure the mass of the contents of a bucket? To find the mass, you have to use math.

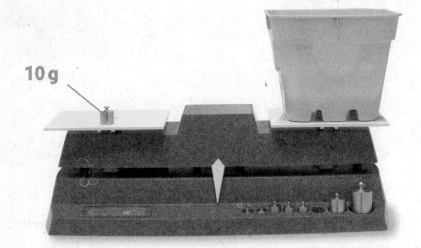

10 g

Find the mass of the container alone. _____

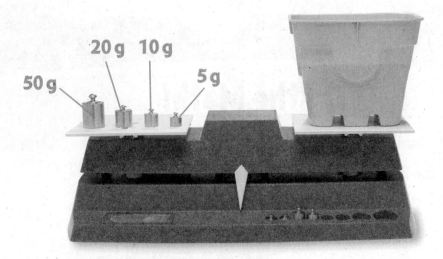

50 g   20 g   10 g   5 g

Find the mass of the container + contents. _____

Now you subtract to find the mass of the contents.

Mass of the container + contents	−	Mass of the container	=	Mass of the contents
_____		_____		_____

What's the Volume?

Matter takes up space. How can you measure the amount of space an object takes up?

Active Reading As you read the next page, circle the name of a tool you can use to measure volume. Underline the units it uses.

An object's **volume** is the amount of space it takes up. To find the volume of a cube or a rectangular [rek•TAN•gyuh•luhr] solid, multiply its length by its width and its height. The length, width, and height of the small cube below are one centimeter.

Do the Math!
Find the Volume

This cube's volume is one cubic centimeter.

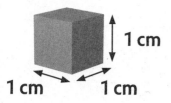

1 cm

1 cm   1 cm

Find the volume of this cube.

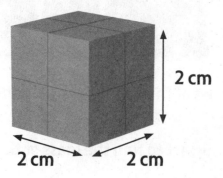

2 cm

2 cm   2 cm

_____ x _____ x _____ = _____ cubic centimeters
   L   W   H

Use a graduated cylinder to measure the volume of a liquid. The units are in milliliters (mL). You can also use it to find the volume of a solid.

Measure It!

Read the level of the water in the graduated cylinder. This is the volume of the water.

_____

Add a shell and read the volume again. This is the volume of the water + the shell.

_____

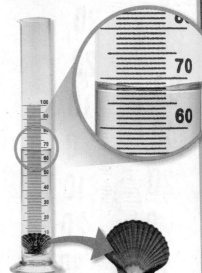

Now subtract to find the volume of the shell. The volume of a solid is measured in cubic centimeters. 1 milliliter equals 1 cubic centimeter, so just change *milliliters* to *cubic centimeters.*

volume of water + shell		volume of water		volume of shell
_____	-	_____	=	_____

Hot and Cold

At the beach, you can feel the difference between hot sand and cold water. How do you measure how warm something is?

Active Reading As you read this page, circle the names of the temperature scales that are being compared.

Temperature is a measure of how warm something is. You use a thermometer to measure temperature.

Thermometers use a scale of numbers to show temperature. There are two scales that are frequently used.

Most weather reports use the Fahrenheit [FAIR•uhn•hyt] scale. On this scale, water becomes ice at 32 degrees. Water boils at 212 degrees.

The other scale is the Celsius [SEL•see•uhs] scale. On this scale, water becomes ice at 0 degrees. Water boils at 100 degrees.

What temperature does the thermometer show?

_____

_____

Measure It!

Write the air temperature and water temperature on the lines. Then color the thermometer to show the temperature of the sand.

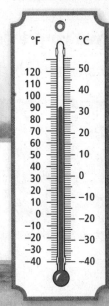

Air Temperature

_____ degrees Celsius

_____ degrees Fahrenheit

You can feel the sand's higher temperature and the water's lower temperature.

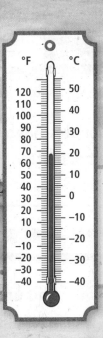

Water Temperature

_____ degrees Celsius

_____ degrees Fahrenheit

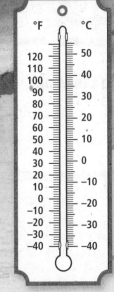

Sand Temperature

The sand's temperature is 37 degrees Celsius. Show that temperature on the thermometer.

When you're done, use the answer key to check and revise your work.

Write the vocabulary term that matches the picture and caption.

1

This crab takes up space and has mass.

_____

2

The blue color is a characteristic of the kite.

_____

3

This manatee has a large amount of matter.

_____

4

This umbrella takes up a lot of space.

_____

5

This thermometer tells how hot it is today.

_____

Answer Key: 1. matter 2. physical property 3. mass 4. volume 5. temperature

Name _____

Word Play

1 Write four words from the box to complete this word web about the physical properties of matter.

| mass | volume | thermometer | color | milliliters | temperature |

◯ _____

◯ _____

◯ _____

◯ _____

(**Physical Properties**)

Apply Concepts

In questions 2-4, write the name of the measurement tool you would use.

 Degrees Celsius   **Milliliters**  **Grams**

Is one drink colder than the other?

_____

Which cup holds the most liquid?

_____

Does a glass of milk have more matter than a glass of punch?

_____

5 Choose an object in your classroom. Write as many physical properties as you can to describe it.

_____

_____

_____

Take It Home!

Share what you have learned about properties of matter with your family. With a family member, name properties of matter at mealtime or in places in your home.

Ask a Metallurgist

gold bars

aluminum foil

Now It's Your Turn!

What properties make steel a good material to use for building bridges?

_____

_____

_____

Q. What is a metallurgist?

A. A metallurgist is a scientist who works with metals. Iron, aluminum, gold, and copper are just some of these metals. They also combine different metals to make a new metal.

Q. Why do they combine different metals?

A. Metals may have different weights, strengths, and hardnesses. They combine metals to change their properties. The new metal may be stronger, harder, or a different color.

Q. How do they use the properties of metals in their work?

A. They look at the properties of metals and how metals can be used. Iron is strong. Mixed with other materials it becomes steel. Steel is a hard and strong metal. Copper can conduct electricity. It's a good metal to use for electrical wires.

copper pennies

This Leads to That

+

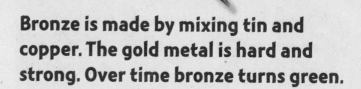

=

Copper is a soft, red metal. It can be shaped into things and over time turns green.

Tin is a silvery-white metal. It's both flexible and brittle.

Bronze is made by mixing tin and copper. The gold metal is hard and strong. Over time bronze turns green.

Compare the properties of copper and bronze. Then complete the table.

Properties of copper	Properties of both	Properties of bronze

Bronze is shaped to make sculptures and bells.

SC.3.N.1.3 Keep records as appropriate, such as pictorial, written, or simple charts and graphs, of investigations conducted.
SC.3.P.8.2 Measure and compare the mass and volume of solids and liquids.

Name _____

Essential Question

How Are Mass and Volume Measured?

Set a Purpose
What skills will you learn?

_____

_____

Think About the Procedure
How can you find the volume of a small object?

_____

_____

_____

When finding the mass of water in a graduated cylinder, why must you first find the mass of the empty graduated cylinder?

_____

_____

_____

Record Your Data
Measure the volume and mass of the water and objects. Make a table to record your results.

Draw Conclusions

When you used water to find the volume of one or more of the objects, how did the volumes of the objects and the water compare?

_____

_____

_____

How did their masses compare?

_____

_____

_____

Analyze and Extend

1. Suppose you have two cubes. They are made of the same material, but one has a greater volume than the other. Does the larger cube have more mass? Explain your answer.

_____

_____

_____

2. A friend collects rocks that fit in the same-sized space in a tray. Could these rocks each have a different volume?

_____

_____

_____

3. When would you have to use a measuring cup to find the volume of a solid?

_____

_____

_____

4. Did all the groups in your class have the same results? How can you explain any differences?

_____

_____

_____

5. Think of other questions you would like to ask about measuring mass and volume.

_____

_____

_____

SC.3.N.1.3 Keep records as appropriate, such as pictorial, written, or simple charts and graphs, of investigations conducted. SC.3.N.1.6 Infer based on observation. SC.3.P.8.1 Measure and compare temperatures of various samples of solids and liquids.

Name _____

Essential Question

How Is Temperature Measured?

Set a Purpose
What skills will you learn from this investigation?

_____

_____

_____

Think About the Procedure
How can you find the temperature of a solid?

_____

_____

_____

_____

Record Your Data
Make a table to record your temperature readings.

Use your temperature measurements to list the substances in order from coolest to warmest.

_____

_____

Draw Conclusions

Some of the objects you tested felt warm and some felt cool. How did this compare with the temperatures you measured?

_____

_____

_____

Analyze and Extend

1. How did the temperatures you measured compare with the temperatures measured by other students? Why?

_____

_____

_____

_____

_____

2. Why is it important to put the thermometer bulb all the way into the liquid or directly in contact with the solid you are measuring?

_____

_____

_____

3. Why do you think cooks use thermometers in the kitchen?

_____

_____

_____

4. How could you find out if the air temperature given in your local weather report is correct?

_____

_____

_____

_____

5. Think of other questions you would like to ask about measuring temperature.

_____

_____

_____

_____

_____

Essential Question

What Are the States of Matter?

Engage Your Brain!

Find the answer to the following question in this lesson and record it here.

How does heating this frozen treat affect it?

_____

_____

Active Reading

Lesson Vocabulary

List the terms, and make notes in the Interactive Glossary as you learn more.

_____

_____

_____

_____

Signal Words: Cause and Effect

Signal words show connections between ideas. Words signaling a cause include *because* and *if*. Words signaling an effect include *so* and *thus*. Active readers remember what they read because they are alert to signal words that identify causes and effects.

What's the State?

What a party! You can eat a piece of solid cake, drink a cold liquid, or play with a gas-filled balloon.

Active Reading As you read these two pages, draw circles around the names of the three states of matter that are being compared.

There are three common states of matter. They are solid, liquid, and gas. Water can be found in all three states.

A **solid** is matter that takes up a definite amount of space. A solid also has a definite shape. Your science book is a solid. Ice is also a solid.

A **liquid** is matter that also takes up a definite amount of space, but it does not have a definite shape. Liquids take the shape of their containers. Drinking water is a liquid.

A **gas** is matter that does not take up a definite amount of space and does not have a definite shape. The air around you is a gas.

curtains _____

ribbon _____

ice cubes _____

orange drink _____

▶ Identify the solids, liquids, and gases in the picture by writing *S, L,* or *G* in each box.

air in balloon _____

bubbles _____

plastic _____

Cool! It's Freezing!

Water freezes at 0 °C.

When matter cools, it loses energy.
How does cooling affect water?

Active Reading As you read these two pages, draw circles around the clue words that signal a cause-and-effect relationship.

All the pictures show water at a temperature lower than 0 degrees Celsius (0 °C) or 32 degrees Fahrenheit (32 °F). How do we know this? If liquid water cools to that temperature, it freezes. Below that temperature, water exists as a solid—ice. Freezing is the change of state from a liquid to a solid.

How would this igloo be different if its temperature was 10 °C?

_____

_____

How can you tell that the temperature of the snow is below 0 °C?

_____

_____

Hail is water that falls to Earth as small balls of ice.

This snowball holds together because the water in it is frozen into a solid.

This girl can skate on ice because ice is a solid.

Do the Math!
Solve a Story Problem

The temperature of a puddle of water is 10 °C. The water cools by two degrees every hour. In how many hours will the puddle of water begin to freeze? Explain how you got your answer.

_____

_____

_____

_____

_____

_____

Just Add Heat!

When matter is heated, it gains energy. How can heating affect water?

Active Reading As you read the next page, draw one line under a cause. Draw two lines under the effect.

Water is a liquid between the temperatures of 0 °C and 100 °C.

If the sun heats this ice sculpture enough, it will begin to melt.

What happens to an ice cube after you take it from the freezer? As it warms, it begins to melt. Melting is the change of state from a solid to a liquid. Ice melts at the same temperature that liquid water freezes—0 °C (32 °F). Melting is the opposite of freezing.

If you heat a pot of water on the stove, the temperature of the water increases until it reaches 100 °C (212 °F). At 100 °C, water boils, or changes rapidly to a gas called *water vapor.* You can't see water vapor. It's invisible.

Water boils at 100 °C.

What's the Temperature?

Draw a line from each thermometer to the picture that shows the state of water indicated by the temperature on the thermometer.

garden hose

ice cube

boiling water

Now You See It . . .

Liquid water can change to a gas without boiling. Look at the drawings of a puddle. What changes do you see?

Water can evaporate at temperatures below 100°C.

Active Reading As you read these two pages, draw a line under each main idea.

Liquid water does not have to boil to become a gas. When you sweat on a hot day, the water on your skin disappears. The liquid water turns into a gas. This is called **evaporation** [ee•vap•uh•RAY•shuhn]. Water can evaporate from other places, such as a puddle.

The sun's heat makes the water in the puddle change to water vapor, which goes into the air.

The puddle gets smaller as the water disappears. Most of the liquid water has changed to a gas.

A gas can change back to a liquid. This is called **condensation** [kahn•duhn•SAY•shuhn]. Water vapor condenses as it cools and loses energy. Water vapor in the air condenses on a cold car window. The outside of a cold soft drink can becomes wet on a hot day. The grass on a cool morning may have dew on it. These are all condensation.

▶ What happened to water vapor in this girl's warm breath as she breathed on the cold window?

_____

_____

_____

Sum It Up!

When you're done, use the answer key to check and revise your work.

Read the statements. Then draw a line to match each statement with the correct picture.

1 This state of matter does not have a definite size or shape.

A

2 This state of matter has a definite size and takes the shape of its container.

B

3 During this process, a liquid changes to a gas.

C

4 This state of matter has a definite size and shape.

D

5 During this process, a gas changes to a liquid.

E

110

Answer Key: 1. E, 2. B, 3. A, 4. C, 5. D

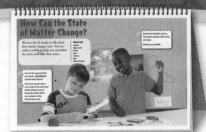
Name _____

SC.3.N.1.3 Keep records as appropriate, such as pictorial, written, or simple charts and graphs, of investigations conducted.
SC.3.P.9.1 Describe the changes water undergoes when it changes state through heating and cooling by using familiar scientific terms such as melting, freezing, boiling, evaporation, and condensation.

Essential Question

How Can the State of Matter Change?

Set a Purpose
What will you learn from this investigation?

_____

_____

_____

Think About the Procedure
How can you show how matter changes state?

_____

_____

_____

Record Your Data
Complete the table below by filling in the missing terms or the missing descriptions of changes in state.

Term	Description of Change
melting	
freezing	
	liquid to gas at 100 °C
evaporation	
	gas to liquid

Draw Conclusions

Write the terms from the table that describe the change from one state to another state.

_ → liquid → solid

_____

_lid → liquid → gas

_____

Analyze and Extend

1. A person wearing eyeglasses leaves an air-conditioned store on a hot day. Her glasses fog up. What change of state happened?

_____

2. Give an example of how freezing affects your everyday life during the summer.

_____

_____

3. A recipe for cookies calls for melted butter. In what state must the butter be?

_____

4. What happens to the volume of liquid water when it boils?

_____

_____

_____

_____

5. A summer rain gets your bike wet. The hot sun comes out. Soon the bike is dry. What happened?

_____

_____

_____

_____

6. Write a question you would like to ask about how matter changes state.

_____

_____

_____

_____

Materials

Cut out these boxes along the dotted lines and use them for your mobile.

Lesson **5**
INQUIRY

1. Water cooling at 0 °C

2. Water at 100 °C

3. Pond water drying up on a hot summer day

4. Ice heated at 0 °C

5. Water appearing on the outside of a cold milk carton on a hot summer day

Multiple Choice

Identify the choice that best answers the question.

SC.3.P.8.1, SC.3.N.1.6

1 Jon measures the temperature of water in four containers. The containers have temperatures of 5 °C, 1 °C, 7 °C, and 0 °C. What can Jon infer about the water?

Ⓐ Two of the containers have solid water in them.

Ⓑ Only one of the containers has solid water in it.

Ⓒ Only two of the containers have liquid water in them.

Ⓓ Only one of the containers has liquid water in it.

SC.3.P.9.1

2 The thermometer shows the temperature outside.

What will happen to an ice cube if you put it outside?

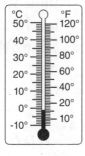

Ⓕ It will not change.

Ⓖ It will change to a gas.

Ⓗ It will change to a solid.

Ⓘ It will change to a liquid.

SC.3.P.8.3, SC.3.N.1.6

3 There are two boxes in a classroom. The first box has a drawing of a long, thin, red object on the outside. Inside it are red pencils, red straws, and red markers. The second box has a drawing of a blue circle on the outside. Which objects would **most likely** be found in the second box?

Ⓐ blue shoes and blue papers

Ⓑ blue golf balls and red CDs

Ⓒ blue marbles and blue plates

Ⓓ blue cups and blue notebooks

SC.3.P.9.1

4 Water changes state during evaporation and condensation. How is evaporation different from condensation?

Ⓕ During evaporation, water changes from a liquid to a gas. During condensation, water changes from a gas to a liquid.

Ⓖ During evaporation, water changes from a gas to a liquid. During condensation, water changes from a liquid to a gas.

Ⓗ During evaporation, water changes from a liquid to a solid. During condensation, water changes from a solid to a liquid.

Ⓘ During evaporation, water changes from a solid to a liquid. During condensation, water changes from a liquid to a solid.

SC.3.P.9.1

5 Yesterday, the temperature of John's pond was −5 °C. Today, the temperature of the pond is 0 °C. Can John ice skate on the pond?

(A) Yes, the pond is solid ice.

(B) No, the pond is liquid water.

(C) No, the pond is starting to condense.

(D) Yes, the pond is made of water vapor.

SC.3.P.8.3, SC.3.N.1.3

6 Onisha wants to sort 20 objects into groups by their color. She wants to record what object was in each group. Which would be the best way to record her sorting?

(F) Draw each of the objects she sorted and staple each drawing into a group.

(G) Make a chart and list the objects into groups the way she sorted them.

(H) Make a bar graph that shows how many objects of each color there are.

(I) List all the objects and put a checkmark by all the blue objects.

SC.3.P.8.2

7 All objects have mass. Which statement about mass is true?

(A) Mass measures how big an object is.

(B) Mass is usually measured in milliliters.

(C) The shape of an object gives it mass.

(D) As matter is added to an object, its mass increases.

SC.3.P.8.2

8 Ben uses a pan balance to compare the masses of two toy blocks. The image below shows Ben's experiment.

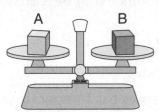

How do the two blocks compare to each other based on the illustration?

(F) Block A has more mass than block B.

(G) Block A has half the mass of block B.

(H) Block A has the same mass as block B.

(I) Block B is darker than block A, so it has more matter.

SC.3.P.8.2, SC.3.N.1.3

9 Rosa measures the volume of four objects. Rosa places each object into a graduated cylinder of water, one at a time. She measures the starting water level and final water level each time. The table below shows Rosa's results.

	Rock	Marble	Golf ball	Bar magnet
Starting water level (mL)	50	50	50	50
Final water level (mL)	60	57	65	62
Volume of object (mL)				

For which object will Rosa record the largest volume?

(A) rock

(B) golf ball

(C) marble

(D) bar magnet

SC.3.P.9.1

10 Sam's mom boils water in a pot on the stove. Which of these describes how the state of water changes when the water begins to boil?

Ⓕ gas to liquid
Ⓖ liquid to gas
Ⓗ liquid to solid
Ⓘ solid to liquid

SC.3.P.9.1

11 Beth and T.J. are studying the properties of water. Beth placed a container with 50 mL of water in a freezer. T.J. placed the same kind of container with 25 mL of water in the same freezer. Which will be the same for both containers of water?

Ⓐ masses of the two containers of frozen water
Ⓑ time it takes the water in each container to freeze
Ⓒ temperature at which the water in each container freezes
Ⓓ amount of space the frozen water in each container takes up

SC.3.P.8.3

12 Grace has a notebook, two pencils, a red folder, and three books in her backpack. How are all the things in Grace's backpack alike?

Ⓕ They are all big.
Ⓖ They are all liquids.
Ⓗ They are all solids.
Ⓘ They are the same size.

SC.3.P.9.1

13 Freezing and melting are opposite processes. Which is the opposite of condensing?

Ⓐ cooling
Ⓑ evaporating
Ⓒ freezing
Ⓓ melting

SC.3.P.8.1, SC.3.N.1.3

14 Min's teacher had the class work in four groups. Each group put a thermometer in a similar cup of water. The groups put their cups near the window in the sunlight. They measured the temperature every 3 minutes for 15 minutes. They wrote the temperatures in the table below.

Time (min)	Group 1	Group 2	Group 3	Group 4
	Temperature (°C)			
0	23	22	23	23
3	23	23	24	23
6	25	24	25	25
9	27	26	25	26
12	28	28	27	28
15	30	28	28	29

What is the **most likely** reason the groups wrote different temperatures in the table?

Ⓕ The cups did not have the same type of water.
Ⓖ Some groups wrote down the wrong temperatures.
Ⓗ The thermometers used by some groups were broken.
Ⓘ The temperatures were a bit different in each cup of water.

SC.3.P.8.2

15 Emma is studying the physical properties of a rock. She puts water in a cylinder, and then puts the rock into the cylinder.

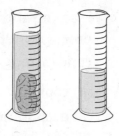

Which of the following properties is Emma measuring?

(A) mass

(B) temperature

(C) texture

(D) volume

SC.3.P.8.3

16 Look at the objects in the picture below.

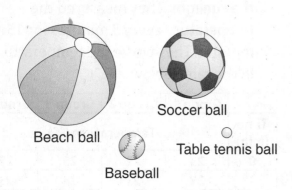

Beach ball

Soccer ball

Baseball

Table tennis ball

Which of the following physical properties is the same for all the balls?

(F) hardness

(G) size

(H) shape

(I) texture

SC.3.P.8.1

17 The temperature in Jessica's house is 24 °C. The temperature outside is 4 °C. Jessica left a bag of marbles on the table outside. What could the temperature of the marbles be after being outside for 15 minutes?

(A) 0 °C

(B) 24 °C

(C) 10 °C

(D) 30 °C

SC.3.P.8.2

18 Tyler puts a ball of clay into a glass of water to find the volume. Next, he flattens the ball into a pancake shape. Then he puts the clay in the water again. What will happen to the clay's volume?

(F) The flat clay's volume will be the same as the round clay's volume.

(G) The flat clay's volume will be one-half of the round clay's volume.

(H) The flat clay's volume will be twice that of the round clay's volume.

(I) The flat clay's volume will be one-fourth of the round clay's volume.

SC.3.P.8.1

19 The temperature of milk in the refrigerator is 5 °C. The temperature of the kitchen is 22 °C. If the milk sits on the kitchen table for 30 minutes, what would its temperature **most likely** be?

(A) 2 °C

(B) 12 °C

(C) 5 °C

(D) 30 °C

SC.3.P.8.2

20 Which of the following balls has the **most** mass?

(F)

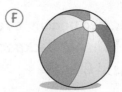

Beach ball

(H)

Bowling ball

(G)

Basketball

(I)

Volleyball

UNIT 4
Forms of Energy

Big Idea 10

Forms of Energy

American Airlines Arena, Miami, Florida

I Wonder Why

Many people like to go to concerts. Why can everyone in this large audience hear the music? *Turn the page to find out.*

Here's Why The arena uses electrical energy to make the sound louder. The sound travels through the air to the audience.

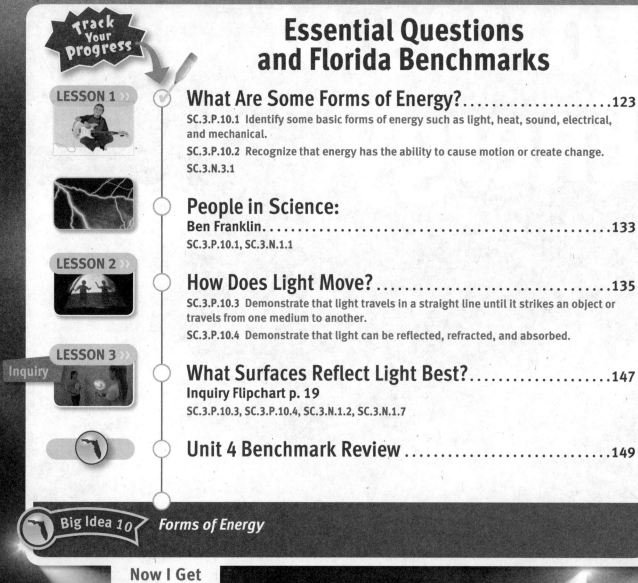

Track Your Progress

Essential Questions and Florida Benchmarks

Big Idea 10 *Forms of Energy*

Now I Get the Big Idea!

SC.3.N.3.1 Recognize that words in science can have different or more specific meanings than their use in everyday language; for example, energy, cell, heat/cold, and evidence. **SC.3.P.10.1** Identify some basic forms of energy such as light, heat, sound, electrical, and mechanical. **SC.3.P.10.2** Recognize that energy has the ability to cause motion or create change.

Essential Question

What Are Some Forms of Energy?

Engage Your Brain!

Find the answer to the following question in this lesson and record it here.

What makes this toy pop up?

_____

_____

_____

_____

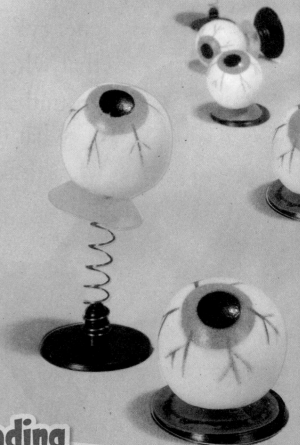

Active Reading

Lesson Vocabulary

List the terms. As you learn about each one, make notes in the Interactive Glossary.

_____ _____

_____ _____

_____

Main Idea

The main idea of a section is the most important idea. The main idea may be stated in the first sentence, or it may be stated elsewhere. Active readers look for main ideas by asking themselves, What is this section mostly about?

What's Energy?

"You have lots of energy!" People say that when you run around a lot. So what is energy?

Active Reading

As you read this page, draw circles around each paragraph's main idea.

Energy is the ability to make something move or change. If you want to put a book on a shelf, it takes energy to move it up there. What about melting snow? It takes energy to change snow to liquid water.

There are many forms of energy. **Potential energy** is stored energy. **Kinetic energy** is the energy of motion. An object can have potential energy, kinetic energy, or both. An object's **mechanical energy** [muh•KAN•ih•kuhl] is the total of its potential energy and kinetic energy.

Potential

The spring gained potential energy when it was pushed down. The ball gained potential energy when it was lifted onto the table.

Kinetic

As the spring and the ball move, their potential energy changes to kinetic energy. The mechanical energy of each stays the same. It just changes form.

▶ Write whether each person or object has potential energy or kinetic energy.

potential

Where's the Energy?

Energy is all around us every day.
It has many different forms.

Active Reading As you read these two pages,
underline the names of forms of energy.

Examine Energy

How do you use energy in your home?
Write an example for each caption.

Sound Energy

Sound comes from the speakers as music.

_____

_____

Electrical Energy

Electrical energy, or electricity [ee•lek•TRIS•ih•tee], is
energy that moves through wires. It makes equipment work.

_____

_____

Heat Energy

Heat from the lights makes the musicians sweat.

_____

_____

Light Energy

Light from the spotlights helps the crowd see the band play.

_____

_____

You use sound energy every day as you talk to your friends and classmates. But think of all the other ways sound energy helps you.

Use Energy

Sound from a whistle gets everyone's attention.

Sound doesn't cook food, but it lets you know when the food is ready.

Sound in the form of music can change your mood!

Do the Math!
Understand Data Tables

Source of Sound	Sound Level
Lawn Mower	90 dB
Mosquito	10 dB
Conversation	60 dB
Hair Dryer	90 dB
Ringing Phone	80 dB
Chainsaw	110 dB

Units called decibels (dB) are used to measure the loudness of sounds. Sounds louder than 85 dB can damage your ears.

1. Which two sources are the safest for your hearing?

_____

2. Which source makes sound that is 25 dB above the safe level?

_____

3. Which two sources give off the same amount of sound?

_____

4. Which source gives off 30 less decibels than the chainsaw?

_____

Sum It Up!

When you're done, use the answer key to check
and revise your work.

Use information in the summary to complete the graphic organizer.

Energy is the ability to move or change something. Potential energy is
stored energy. Kinetic energy is the energy of movement. An object
may have both kinetic and potential energy. The total of these is its
mechanical energy. Any form of energy can change into another form.

1 Main idea: Energy is _____
_____

2 Detail: Potential
energy is
_____
_____.

3 Detail:
_____
_____
is the energy of
movement.

4 Detail: The total of an
object's _____
and _____
_____ is
its _____
_____.

5 Pick two forms of energy. Then write
an example of one way you use each one.

_____

_____

6 _____

_____

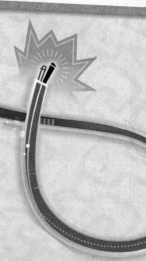

Answer Key: 1. the ability to move or change something **2.** stored
energy **4.** kinetic; potential energy; mechanical energy **3.** kinetic
energy **4.** kinetic; potential energy; mechanical energy **5.** heat energy; cooking food
6. sound energy; knowing when school lets out

Brain Check

Name _____

Word Play

1 Unscramble each word and write it in the boxes.

1. GEERNY
   This lesson is about different forms of _____.
   [ ][ ][ ][⊙][ ]

2. LAPNETOTI
   Stored energy
   [ ][ ][⊙][ ][ ][ ][⊙][ ]

3. LLEERCTIAC
   A form of energy that moves through wires
   [ ][⊙][ ][⊙][ ][ ][⊙][ ][⊙]

4. ITINECK
   The energy of motion
   [ ][⊙][ ][⊙][ ][⊙]

5. ATHE
   A form of energy you can feel from the sun
   [⊙][ ][⊙][ ]

6. NUODS
   A form of energy that might wake you up in the morning
   [ ][ ][ ][⊙][ ]

7. EVMO
   Energy is the ability to make something do this.
   [⊙][ ][ ][ ]

8. GNCAHE
   Energy is also the ability to make something do this.
   [ ][⊙][ ][ ][ ][ ]

Write the letters in the circles here.
Unscramble them to form two more words.

_ _ _ _ _ _ _ _ _ _ _ _ _ _

9. The energy that is a total of # 2 and #4
   [ ][ ][ ][ ][ ][ ][ ][ ][ ][ ]

10. A form of energy you can see that comes from the sun
    [ ][ ][ ][ ][ ]

Apply Concepts

Write the form of energy each object takes in.

 2

_____

3

_____

Write the form of energy each object produces.

4

_____

5

_____

_____

 With your family, go through your house and look for things that use or produce the following kinds of energy: light, sound, heat, and electrical. Identify two items for each kind of energy.

Take It Home!

132

SC.3.N.1.1 Raise questions about the natural world, investigate them individually and in teams through free exploration and systematic investigations, and generate appropriate explanations based on those explorations. SC.3.P.10.1 Identify some basic forms of energy such as light, heat, sound, electrical, and mechanical.

Learn About ...

Benjamin Franklin

Benjamin Franklin was born in January 1706. He moved from Boston to Philadelphia in 1723. Franklin worked as a printer and made newspapers. Later, he became a scientist and an inventor. He discovered that lightning is a form of electricity. In 1752, Franklin flew a kite in a rainstorm. A wire on the kite attracted electricity in the cloud. The electricity went down the string to a metal key. Scientists still study electricity today.

Fun Fact

Did you know that Franklin once used a kite to pull him while swimming?

Read the timeline below. Use what you read about Benjamin Franklin to fill in each blank box.

1750 Franklin invents the lightning rod to protect buildings from lightning.

1706 Franklin is born in Boston, Massachusetts.

Think About It!

In what ways does electricity make our lives easier?

_____

_____

_____

_____

SC.3.P.10.3 Demonstrate that light travels in a straight line until it strikes an object or travels from one medium to another. **SC.3.P.10.4** Demonstrate that light can be reflected, refracted, and absorbed.

Essential Question

How Does Light Move?

🧠 Engage Your Brain!

Find the answer to the following question in this lesson and record it here.

What's wrong with the writing on the ambulance? It's backwards! Why?

_____

_____

_____

_____

Active Reading

Lesson Vocabulary

List the terms. As you learn about each, make notes in the Interactive Glossary.

_____

_____

_____

Cause and Effect

Signal words show connections between ideas. Words signaling a cause include *because* and *if*. Words signaling an effect include *so* and *thus*. Active readers remember what they read because they are alert to signal words that identify causes and effects.

A Lighted Path

Light is all around us. Light's movement allows us to see. How?

Active Reading As you read these two pages, draw a circle around the clue word that signals a cause.

Light moves in straight lines. In the picture at the top of this page, the flashlight beam is a straight line. The beam does not bend or curve. Look at the picture below. The top of the light beam is a straight line, and the bottom of the light beam is a straight line. The whole light beam is straight.

The light is below the boy's face. The shadow of his nose is above his nose.

What happens when light hits an object? It cannot keep going straight.

Objects can absorb light. **Absorb** means to take in. The marshmallow and the stick block light. They either absorb or bounce back all of the light that hits them. No light goes through.

The marshmallow and stick have a shadow. A **shadow** is the dark area behind an object that has blocked light. The shadow has a shape that is similar to the object. That's because light travels in straight lines.

The light in the tent is blocked by the kids' bodies. They absorb most of the light that hits them. You can see the shadows on the side of the tent.

▶ One of these lights is on. It is making a shadow behind the block. Draw a circle around the light that is on.

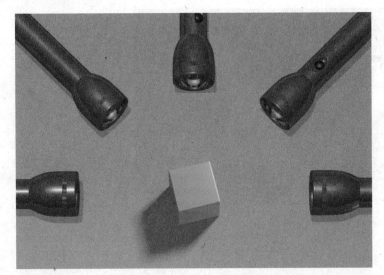

Seeing Double

Not all objects absorb light. Some objects bounce light back in the opposite direction.

A surface can **reflect**, or bounce back, light. Smooth glass, metal, and water reflect well. Picture a calm lake. The image on the lake is formed by light reflecting off its surface.

The beam of the flashlight below is shining downward. It traveled in a straight line until it hit an object that reflected it. The light bounced back up when it reflected.

Did you ever notice that things look backward in a mirror? Words are hard to read if you reflect them in a mirror because they're reversed. A reflected image is always reversed.

Use a hand mirror to read this sign. What does it say?

_____

▶ Draw the reflection of the canoe in the water.

Bend It!

Glass and water can reflect light. They can also bend light.

Active Reading As you read these two pages, underline the definition of *refract*.

Refraction quacks me up!

refraction

Light can **refract**, or bend, when it moves from one clear material to another. When the beam hits the water in the tank, it refracts.

▶ Fill in the cause. Then circle the place in the photo where refraction occurs.

Cause

→

Effect

_____

_____

An object may appear broken

refraction

It's easy to see where light is refracted. Just look for the break! What makes the duck look broken? Light reflects from the duck above water and underwater. Light from the duck's top half goes straight to your eyes. Light from its bottom half goes through water first. The light refracts as it leaves the water. This makes the duck's belly and legs look separated from the top half of its body!

Reflection and Refraction

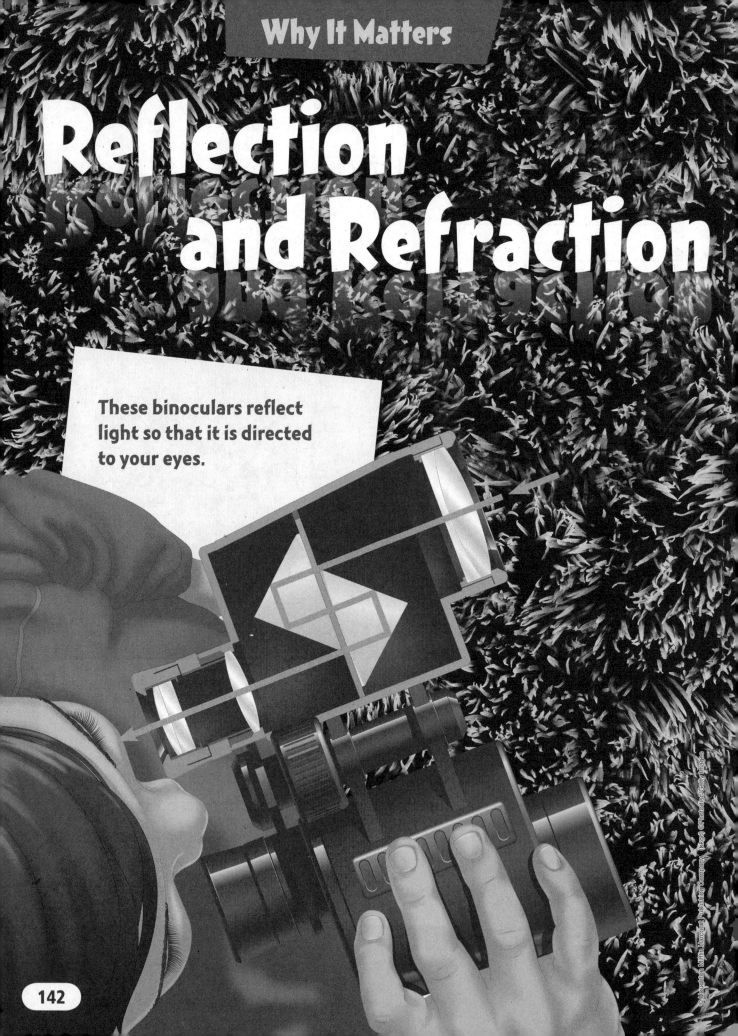

These binoculars reflect light so that it is directed to your eyes.

The lenses in this telescope refract light. This makes the object seem larger. Lenses in binoculars also refract light to make objects look larger.

If light didn't reflect, you'd never be able to see yourself in a mirror. If light didn't refract, there would be no telescopes, cameras, microscopes, or eyeglasses.

All of these items use lenses. Their lenses are made to refract. Items such as these depend on refracting lenses to work.

Do the Math!
Multiply Whole Numbers

Tom watches a robin. It appears about three inches in size. He then watches it through binoculars. The robin now appears to be nine inches in size. How many times as large did the robin look through the binoculars?

When you're done, use the answer key to check
and revise your work.

**Finish the summary statements. Then draw a line
to match each statement with the correct image.**

1 When light passes through a
clear material, it bends, or
_____ .

2 Some objects take in, or
_____ light.

3 Behind an object that absorbs
light, you will see a dark spot
called a _____ .

4 When light hits a shiny surface,
it bounces back, or
_____ .

5 Light travels in a
_____ path.

Answer Key: 1. refracts; connect to glass with straw ; 2. absorbs; connect to rocks;
3. shadow; connect to boy with shadow; 4. reflects; connect to flashlight beam
reflecting off mirror ; 5. straight; connect to flashlight

Name _____

Word Play

1 Use the words in the box to complete the puzzle.

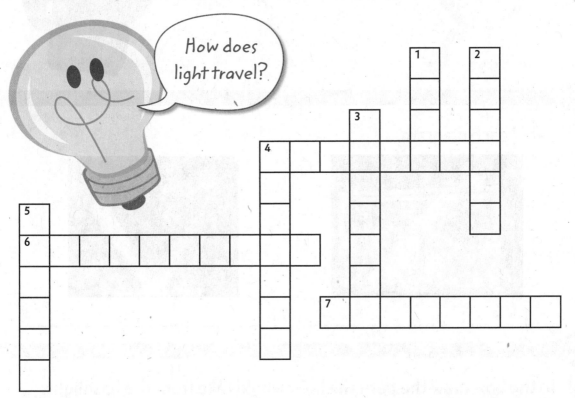

How does light travel?

Down

1. Its purpose is to refract light.
2. An area that light cannot reach
3. To bounce back in the opposite direction
4. Bend, as light does when it moves from air to water
5. Marshmallows reflect and _____ light when it hits them.

Across

4. Objects in mirrors look like this
6. Uses lenses to reflect and refract light
7. The kind of path light travels in

| absorb* | binoculars | lens | reflect* | refract* | reversed |
| shadow* | straight |

* Key Lesson Vocabulary

Apply Concepts

2 Draw a circle around the item that reflects light. Draw a square around the item that refracts light. Draw a triangle around the item that absorbs light.

3 Label each diagram.

_____   _____

4 In the box, draw the path the light would take from the flashlight.

Take It Home!

With your family, go through your home, looking for two things that reflect light, two things that refract light, and two things that absorb light.

SC.3.N.1.2 Compare the observations made by different groups... **SC.3.N.1.7** Explain that empirical evidence is information...that is used to help validate explanations of natural phenomena. **SC.3.P.10.3** Demonstrate that light travels in a straight line until it strikes an object or travels from one medium to another. **SC.3.P.10.4** Demonstrate that light can be reflected, refracted, and absorbed.

Name _____

Essential Question

What Surfaces Reflect Light Best?

Set a Purpose
What will you learn from this experiment?

_____

_____

_____

_____

State Your Hypothesis
Write your hypothesis, or testable statement.

_____

_____

_____

Think About the Procedure
What is the tested variable?

_____

Why should you use the same light source with each object?

_____

_____

_____

_____

Record Your Data
Record your setup and results in the boxes below and on the next page. Use one box for each object tested.

2. Why do you think some objects did not reflect light onto the wall?

_____

_____

_____

_____

3. What similarities, if any, did you observe in the way the objects responded to the light?

_____

_____

_____

_____

4. Think of other questions you would like to ask about things that reflect light.

_____

_____

_____

_____

Draw Conclusions

What can you conclude about the way shiny and dull objects respond to light?

_____

_____

_____

Analyze and Extend

1. Can you think of a real-life situation that supports your conclusion?

_____

_____

Name _____

Multiple Choice

Identify the choice that best answers the question.

SC.3.P.10.1

1 There are different types of energy. Which item is an example of electrical energy?

(A)

(C)

(B)

(D)

SC.3.P.10.2

2 Kendall feels tired after riding his bicycle. He uses a blender to make a health shake. Which types of energy are used and output by the blender?

(F) electrical; heat and light
(G) electrical; potential and heat
(H) electrical; kinetic and sound
(I) mechanical; sound and potential

SC.3.P.10.1

3 Dan turns off an electric fan, a flashlight, a lamp, and the television. Which one gives off both light and sound energy?

(A) electric fan   (C) lamp
(B) flashlight   (D) television

SC.3.P.10.2

4 Students are enjoying a field trip. They see activities that involve different types of energy. Edie is looking at the archery exhibit.

Which explanation tells what happens when the girl lets go of the bow?

(F) Potential energy becomes kinetic energy.
(G) Kinetic energy becomes potential energy.
(H) Mechanical energy becomes light energy.
(I) Mechanical energy becomes electrical energy.

SC.3.P.10.3

5 On a sunny day, Jamil sits under the shade of a tree. Which of the following describes the area under the tree?

(A) cooler and darker
(B) cooler and brighter
(C) warmer and darker
(D) warmer and brighter

SC.3.P.10.1

6 Midori's mom heats bread in an electric toaster oven. As it heats, the coils inside the oven glow. The oven beeps when the bread is done. The oven uses different types of energy. Study the chart below.

A	heat
B	light
C	electrical
D	sound

Which types of energy are present during this process?

F A only
G A and B only
H A, B, and C only
I A, B, C, and D

SC.3.P.10.3, SC.3.N.1.2

7 A light meter measures how much light is given off. Javier and Lucas measure light from a flashlight. Javier stands next to the flashlight. Lucas stands one meter away. They place their meters in the beam of light. Javier's meter registers more light. Why?

A Javier's meter blocked some of the light from reaching Lucas' meter.
B Lucas' meter blocked some of the light from reaching Javier's meter.
C The light traveled in a curved line, so it did not shine on Lucas' meter.
D Lucas read the meter wrong, and they both had the same reading.

SC.3.P.10.1

8 Energy is used during sporting events. Sometimes it is used by the players and sometimes it is used by the equipment. Which is an example of kinetic energy?

F soccer player kicking a ball
G skier perched at the top of a hill
H football player standing by an outdoor heater
I lights used when taking a picture of a winning runner

SC.3.P.10.4

9 Mia pointed a flashlight straight ahead. The light traveled forward. Then it suddenly traveled straight back at Mia. Which of the following objects did the light **most** likely strike?

A brick wall
B large mirror
C clear glass window
D frosted glass window

SC.3.P.10.4

10 Damon has a watch with a solar panel on it. The solar panel stores energy from sunlight. Which of the following **most** likely happens when sunlight strikes the solar panel?

F Sunlight is reflected.
G Sunlight is refracted.
H Sunlight is absorbed.
I Sunlight is transmitted.

SC.3.P.10.2, SC.3.P.10.4

11 Drew and Amy each took a glass and placed water in it. Drew used faucet water, and Amy used water from a fountain. They wrapped their glasses with white paper, and placed them under a light. The temperatures after 20 minutes are shown below.

Cup	Temperature (°C)
Drew's cup	30
Amy's cup	25

What might explain the difference in Drew's and Amy's temperatures?

Ⓐ Drew's water evaporated, and Amy's did not.

Ⓑ Drew used a different color of paper than Amy did.

Ⓒ Drew's starting temperature was different from Amy's.

Ⓓ Drew's water was placed under a light, and Amy's water was in the shade.

SC.3.P.10.2, SC.3.N.3.1

12 Raul sits at his desk to study. On his desk are a drinking glass, lamp, fan, and books. Based on the way the term *energy* is used in science, which of these is true?

Ⓕ The books have kinetic energy.

Ⓖ The glass has potential energy.

Ⓗ The lamp has sound energy.

Ⓘ The fan has light energy.

SC.3.P.10.3

13 Rylee and Ming each hold an end of a bent hollow tube. They shine a light through the end, but cannot see it at the other end of the tube. Which tells why they cannot see the light?

Ⓐ The light that they are using is too dim, so it cannot travel that far.

Ⓑ Light travels in a straight line. The tube is bent, so it absorbs the light.

Ⓒ The tube is too dark. If they try a lighter tube, the light will show up.

Ⓓ The openings are not large enough to allow the light to enter and exit.

SC.3.P.10.4

14 Blake is standing in a pond looking at fish. From above the water, they look large. From under the water, they look smaller. What happens to light as it travels from the water to the air?

Ⓕ It stops.   Ⓗ It reflects.

Ⓖ It bends.   Ⓘ It is absorbed.

SC.3.P.10.2

15 Sammy places jeans into an electric clothes dryer and pushes the power button. Which explanation tells what happens in the dryer?

Ⓐ Electrical energy changes into heat energy.

Ⓑ Electrical energy changes into potential energy.

Ⓒ Potential energy changes into electrical energy.

Ⓓ Mechanical energy changes into electrical energy

SC.3.P.10.4, SC.3.N.1.3

16 Lillian placed red and black paper on the sidewalk. She placed a thermometer on each piece of paper. She then recorded the temperature every 2 minutes. What is the **best** way to keep a record so she can compare the temperatures later?

(F) a table of the colors

(G) a drawing of the experiment

(H) a graph of the temperatures

(I) a list of the hourly air temperatures in her neighborhood

SC.3.P.10.3

17 Diane is planning to make shadow puppets with her hands. She places a lamp and a white screen as shown below.

Screen

Lamp

Where should Diane stand to make the shapes with her hands?

(A) behind the lamp

(B) behind the screen

(C) on any of the sides of the lamp

(D) between the lamp and the screen

SC.3.P.10.2, SC.3.N.1.2

18 A class used a fan's energy to blow a piece of paper. Groups then measured how far the paper moved. Group A said the paper moved 35 cm. Group B said the paper moved 32 cm. Why might they have gotten different answers?

(F) The paper was not small enough.

(G) One of the rulers was shorter than the other.

(H) The groups used different units.

(I) One of the groups misread the measurement from the ruler.

SC.3.P.10.3, SC.3.N.1.7

19 Maria entered a dark room. She shined a flashlight on a chair. What could she observe as evidence that the chair absorbed the light?

(A) The light was not very bright.

(B) The light traveled in a curved line.

(C) The light traveled in a straight line.

(D) The light did not go through the chair.

SC.3.P.10.2, SC.3.N.1.7

20 A ball falls off a shelf. What is the evidence that it has energy as it falls?

(F) The ball is round, and all round objects have energy.

(G) The ball is moving, and things that are moving have energy.

(H) The ball is very heavy, and energy is what gives objects weight.

(I) The ball is falling toward Earth, and energy pulls objects toward Earth.

Heat Sources

Big Idea 11

Energy Transfer and Transformations

Lightning strikes over Miami, Florida

I Wonder Why

Lightning is bright. But lightning also sometimes starts fires. Why? *Turn the page to find out.*

Here's Why Lightning gives off light, but it also gives off heat. The temperature of a lightning bolt can be hotter than the surface of the sun! No wonder it can set things on fire.

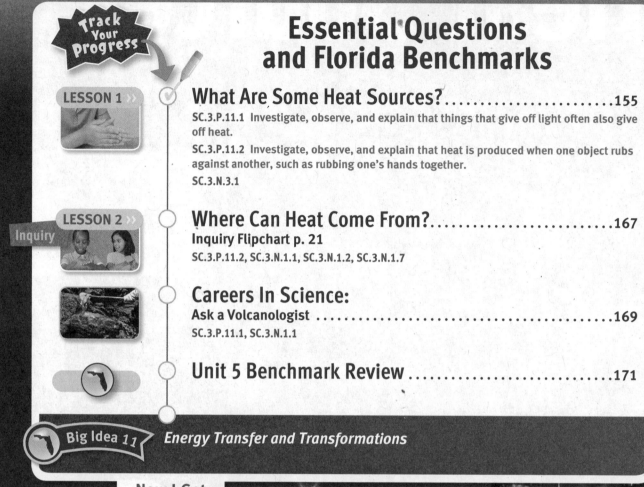

Track Your Progress

Essential Questions and Florida Benchmarks

Big Idea 11 *Energy Transfer and Transformations*

Now I Get the Big Idea!

SC.3.N.3.1 Recognize that words in science can have different or more specific meanings than their use in everyday language; for example, energy, cell, heat/cold, and evidence. SC.3.P.11.1 Investigate, observe, and explain that things that give off light often also give off heat. SC.3.P.11.2 Investigate, observe, and explain that heat is produced when one object rubs against another, such as rubbing one's hands together.

Essential Question

What Are Some Heat Sources?

Engage Your Brain!

Find the answer to the following question in this lesson and record it here.

The brakes on a car rub against the wheels to stop the car. But why are this car's brakes bright orange?

_____

_____

_____

Active Reading

Lesson Vocabulary
List the terms. As you learn about each one, make notes in the Interactive Glossary.

_____

_____

Main Idea
The main idea of a section is the most important idea. The main idea may be stated in the first sentence, or it may be stated elsewhere. Active readers look for main ideas by asking themselves, What is this section mostly about?

Sharing the Warmth

Here are two common words: heat and temperature. You hear them every day. But what do they really mean?

Active Reading As you read these two pages, circle the clue word or phrase that signals a detail such as an example or an added fact.

Scientists use words very carefully. Some common words have special meanings in science. For example, when you use the word *heat*, you might mean how warm something is. In science, **heat** is energy that moves from warmer objects to cooler objects.

The temperature of the water in these hot springs is higher than the temperature of the monkeys. Heat flows from the warmer water to the monkeys. The monkeys feel warmer.

Temperature is the measure of how hot or cold something is. Temperature can be measured in degrees. Water with a temperature of 32 °C (90 °F) is hotter than water with a temperature of 12 °C (54 °F).

Remember, heat is energy. Heat always moves from an object with a higher temperature to one with a lower temperature.

Heat Can Move

In each picture, heat will flow from one object to another. Draw an arrow to show which way it will flow.

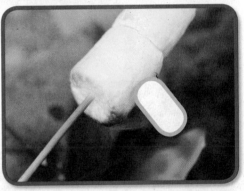

The red part of the metal horseshoe has a very high temperature. Heat moved from the fire into the red part of the horseshoe.

Turn Up the Heat

Heat moves from something warmer to something cooler. You rely on that every day. How? Here is just one way.

Would you like to eat nothing but raw food? Ugh! For things to cook, they must gain heat energy.

Heat moves from the blue flames to the pot. Then it moves from the pot to the stew. The heat cooks the stew.

1. This oven is used to bake food. Heat moves from the oven to the air inside the oven. Then it moves from the hot air to the food. The heat from the oven baked these cookies!

2. Some things slow the movement of heat. The woman in the picture is using oven mitts. The mitts slow the movement of heat, so she does not get burned.

Do the Math!

Read a Table

1. What foods are cooked at 145 °F?

_____

2. Which food needs to be cooked at a higher temperature, eggs or chicken?

_____

3. What food is cooked at 160 °F?

_____

Safe Food Cooking Temperatures

Type of Food	Cooking Temperature
Eggs	160 °F
Salmon	145 °F
Beef	145 °F
Chicken	165 °F

Hot Light

Old-fashioned light bulbs give off heat. Some newer kinds give off more light and less heat.

Have you ever touched a light bulb that had been on for a while? The heat may have surprised you!

Active Reading As you read these two pages, draw a star next to what you consider to be the most important sentence, and be ready to explain why.

You've learned that heat is energy. But remember, light is a form of energy, too. Heat and light often occur together. Many things that give off light also often give off heat.

The light bulb is used for its light, but it also gives off heat. The coil inside a toaster gives off heat. That's how the bread gets toasted. But the coil also gives off an orange-red light. When something gives off both light and heat, we often want to use just one or the other.

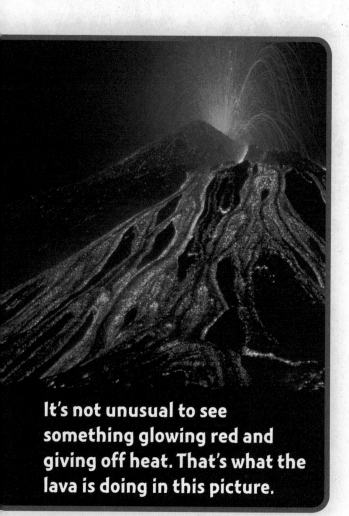

It's not unusual to see something glowing red and giving off heat. That's what the lava is doing in this picture.

The sun gives off light, and it also gives off heat. We need both to survive.

Heat and Light Sources

How many things in your house give off light and heat? List some of them here.

_____

_____

_____

_____

The charcoal is giving off orange light. It also gives off the heat that cooks the meat.

The light from a candle's flame can let us see in a dark room. The heat from the flame melts the wax.

Burn Rubber

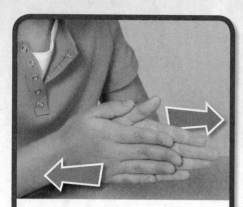

If you're ever out in the cold without gloves, rub your hands together. The heat you produce will warm your hands!

Q: Can you make a fire by rubbing two sticks together?
A: Yes, if one of them is a match!

That's an old joke, so you may have heard it before. However, you actually can make a fire by rubbing two sticks together. You have to move them quickly, and you must have something nearby to burn. But it can be done. Where do you think the heat comes from?

Active Reading As you read these two pages, draw circles around two words or phrases that are key to understanding the main idea.

The tires are rubbing against the road as they spin. They're spinning very quickly and producing a lot of heat. They're getting so hot that they're burning. That's where the smoke is coming from.

© Houghton Mifflin Harcourt Publishing Company (t) © Getty Images/PhotoDisc; (b) © Lyle Owerko/Reportage/Getty Images

When two things rub against each other, there is *friction* [FRIK•shuhn] where they touch. Friction produces heat. The faster and harder the two things rub, the more heat is produced.

Where Is Heat Produced?

In each photo, two things are rubbing together to produce heat. Draw a circle around the point where the heat is being produced. Then write a caption for each picture.

Sum It Up!

When you're done, use the answer key to check
and revise your work.

Write the correct word in the blank.

1 Things that give off

_____

often give off heat as well.

2

_____

is measured in degrees.

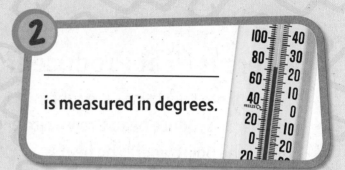

Complete the graphic organizer.

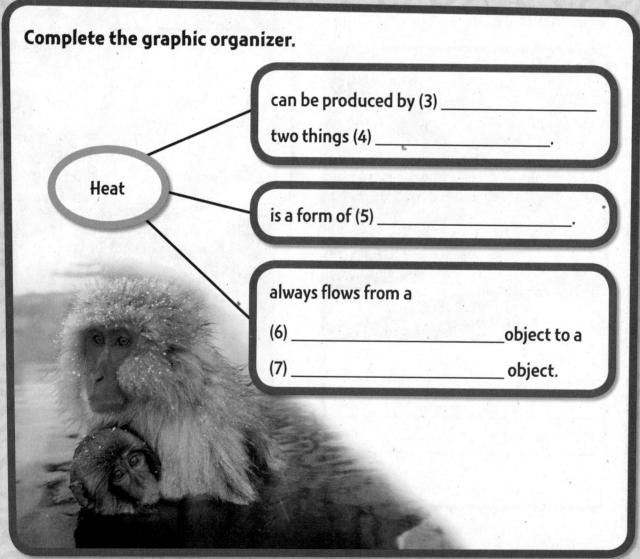

Heat

can be produced by (3) _____

two things (4) _____.

is a form of (5) _____.

always flows from a

(6) _____ object to a

(7) _____ object.

Brain Check

Name _____

Word Play

1 Use the clues to help unscramble each word. Write the unscrambled word in the boxes.

Something with a higher temperature is

E T H O T R

☐ ☐ ☐ ☐ ⊙ ☐

Something that is hot may do this.

W L G O

⊙ ☐ ☐ ☐

The measure of how hot or cold something is

M T E E E R P U T A R

☐ ☐ ☐ ☐ ⊙ ☐ ☐ ☐ ☐ ☐ ☐

Friction from spinning race car tires might cause this.

M K S O E

⊙ ☐ ☐ ☐ ⊙

This produces heat when two things rub together.

I T R N F I C O

☐ ⊙ ☐ ☐ ☐ ☐ ☐ ☐

Something with a very low temperature is this.

O C D L

☐ ☐ ☐ ⊙

Unscramble the letters in the circles to form a word that is related to this lesson.

☐ ☐ ☐ ☐ ☐ ☐

Apply Concepts

2 Circle the object that can give off heat but not light.

sun

candle

hot chocolate

3 Name two things you sometimes do to prevent heat from being transferred.

_____

_____

_____

4 Name two things that give off both light and heat.

_____

5 Name one way that you use heat.

_____

Take It Home!

With your family, pick two rooms in your home. Go through the rooms, looking for everything that produces light. For each thing you find, discuss if that thing also produces heat.

SC.3.N.1.1 Raise questions about the natural world...generate appropriate explanations based on those explorations. SC.3.N.1.2 Compare the observations made by different groups...to explain the differences across groups. SC.3.N.1.7 Explain that empirical evidence is information...that is used to help validate explanations of natural phenomena. SC.3.P.11.2 Investigate, observe, and explain that heat is produced when one object rubs against another, such as rubbing one's hands together.

Name _____

Essential Question

Where Can Heat Come From?

Set a Purpose

What do you think is the purpose of this investigation?

_____

_____

_____

_____

Think About the Procedure

Why are you using different items to rub together?

_____

_____

_____

Record Your Data

Record your results in the table below.

Setup	Hot?	Observations
hands rubbed against each other		
cloths rubbed against each other		
paper rubbed against **wood** with **nothing** between them		
paper rubbed against **wood** with **dish soap** between them		

Draw Conclusions

Compare your results with the other groups. What do you find?

_____

_____

Why might this be the case?

_____

_____

Analyze and Extend

1. If two parts of a machine rub together, what could you do to keep them from getting as hot?

_____

_____

_____

_____

2. How would you plan an investigation to find possible materials to reduce friction?

_____

_____

_____

_____

_____

_____

3. Look at the setup below. Ramp 1 has a smooth surface. Ramp 2 has a sandpaper surface. Will the book on either ramp move? Explain.

Ramp 1

Ramp 2

_____

_____

_____

_____

_____

4. What other questions would you like to ask about how heat can be produced?

_____

_____

_____

_____

SC.3.N.1.1 Raise questions about the natural world...and generate appropriate explanations based on those explorations. **SC.3.P.11.1** Investigate, observe, and explain that things that give off light often also give off heat.

Ask a Volcanologist

Q. What does a volcanologist do?

A. A volcanologist is a person who studies volcanoes. We can warn people when a volcano will erupt. People will have time to get to safety.

Q. How do you stay safe when working around lava?

A. I wear special clothes, gloves, and boots to protect me from the heat. I wear a gas mask to protect me from volcanic gases.

Q. How do you know that lava is very hot?

A. Lava is very hot! You know that lava is hot because it gives off heat and light. It may glow bright orange, yellow, or red.

Now It's Your Turn!

What question would you ask a volcanologist?

_____

_____

_____

_____

Be a Volcanologist

Volcanologists can tell lava's temperature by the color it glows.

Match each temperature below to the lava flowing from the volcano. Write the temperature in the correct location.

1100°C	bright orange
850°C	bright red
650°C	dark red
200°C	black

Volcano

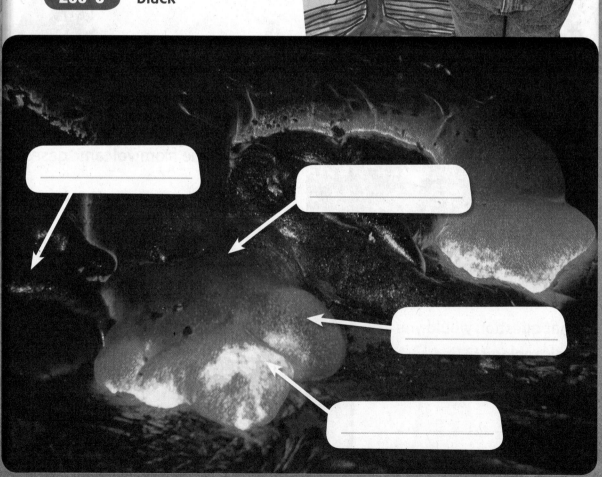

Name _____

Multiple Choice

Identify the choice that best answers the question.

SC.3.P.11.1

1 Sandra's mother is boiling water on a stove. In which picture does the arrow show the direction that heat moves to make the water boil?

Ⓐ

Ⓑ

Ⓒ

Ⓓ

SC.3.P.11.1

2 Hiroto wants to warm a pot of soup on a stove. He will put the pot onto one of the stove's heat elements and turn it on .

Heat elements

Which heat element does Hiroto know is very hot, without touching them?

Ⓕ the biggest one

Ⓖ the smallest one

Ⓗ the one that glows red

Ⓘ the one that looks dark

SC.3.P.11.1

3 Lucas is having a birthday party. He has ice cream, balloons, and a cake with candles.

Which of the objects shown in the picture produces the most heat?

Ⓐ cake
Ⓑ candles
Ⓒ balloon
Ⓓ ice cream

SC.3.P.11.2

4 Nolan picks up a book from his desk and hands it to his teacher. His teacher sets the book down and slides it across a table. Which action produces the most heat?

Ⓕ sliding the book across a table
Ⓖ handing the book to his teacher
Ⓗ setting the book down on a table
Ⓘ picking the book up from his desk

SC.3.P.11.1, SC.3.N.1.2

5 Marvin and Byron both hold a thermometer close to a light bulb. After 2 minutes, they record their measurement. Marvin records 67 °C. Byron records 65 °C. Why might they have different results?

Ⓐ The light bulb is not the same temperature on all sides.
Ⓑ Marvin held his thermometer closer to the bulb than Byron did.
Ⓒ One of the thermometers was not working correctly.
Ⓓ Marvin read the Fahrenheit temperature instead of the Celsius temperature.

SC.3.P.11.1

6 Jamal is toasting marshmallows over a campfire.

Which of the following signs shows that the fire is probably hot?

Ⓕ It has sticks in it.
Ⓖ It has bright flames.
Ⓗ It has ashes around it.
Ⓘ It has sand under the logs.

SC.3.P.11.2

7 A mover pushes a box up a ramp into a truck.

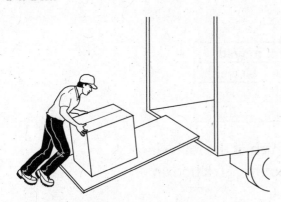

Which two things become warmer when the man pushes the box?

- Ⓐ box and air
- Ⓑ ramp and box
- Ⓒ man and truck
- Ⓓ truck and ramp

SC.3.P.11.2, SC.3.N.3.1

8 Jason is sanding a board with sandpaper. He puts a piece of sandpaper around a block of wood and sands the board. Which of the following terms has a specific meaning in science that could relate to Jason's activity?

- Ⓕ experiment
- Ⓖ evidence
- Ⓗ heat
- Ⓘ sanding

SC.3.P.11.2, SC.3.N.1.1

9 Matthew's class investigates friction between smooth items and rough items. They find that rough items produce more friction. Which of the following items would create the most heat if rubbed together for 20 seconds?

Ⓐ

Plastic containers

Ⓑ
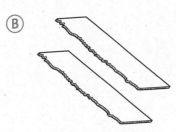
Rough cardboard

Ⓒ
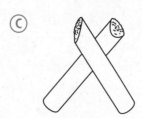
Chalk

Ⓓ
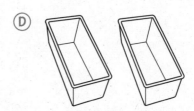
Baking pans

SC.3.P.11.2, SC.3.N.1.7

10 Jenna and Tanner want to decrease the friction between a wooden block and a ramp. They have tried two objects already and will try others.

Ramp covering	How object moved	
	Faster	Slower
Plastic tablecloth	X	
Cloth tablecloth		X

Based on the evidence they have gathered, which of the following choices are **most likely** to create the least amount of friction on the ramp?

(F) carpet

(G) bed sheet

(H) plastic cover

(I) curtain

Plants and the Environment

Big Idea 14

Organization and Development of Living Organisms

Marie Selby Botanical Gardens, Sarasota, Florida

I Wonder Why

Like animals, plants are living things. But most plants can't eat food. Why do they survive? *Turn the page to find out.*

Here's Why Plants can make their own food. They use sunlight, air, and water to make food. This process takes place in their leaves.

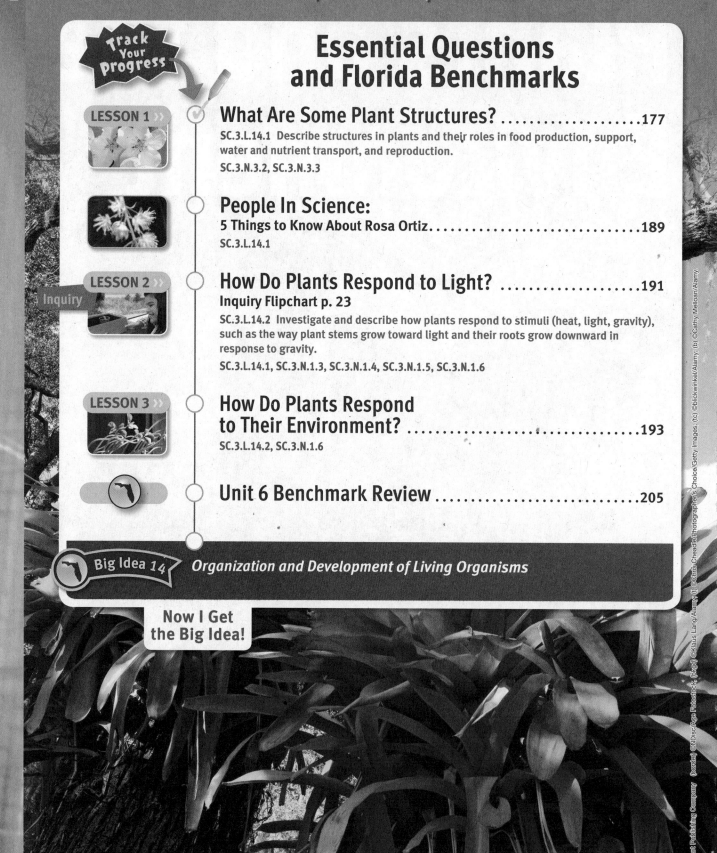

Track Your Progress

Essential Questions and Florida Benchmarks

Big Idea 14 *Organization and Development of Living Organisms*

Now I Get the Big Idea!

SC.3.L.14.1 Describe structures in plants and their roles in food production, support, water and nutrient transport, and reproduction.

Lesson 1

Essential Question

What Are Some Plant Structures?

Engage Your Brain!

Find the answer to the following question in this lesson and record it here.

What do the roots at the bottom of this plant do for the plant?

_____

_____

Active Reading

Lesson Vocabulary

List the terms. As you learn about each one, make notes in the Interactive Glossary.

_____ _____

_____ _____

Sequence

Many of the ideas in this lesson are connected by a sequence, or order, that describes the steps in a process. Active readers stay focused on sequence when they mark the transition from one step in a process to another.

Get to the Bottom of It

Plants come in many shapes and sizes. Did you know that an important part of most plants is hidden underground?

Active Reading As you read this page, circle lesson vocabulary words when they are defined.

Plants are made up of different parts. Each part has a function that helps the plant grow and survive.

The part of the carrot plant that we eat is its root. Roots hold plants in the ground. Roots also take in, or absorb [uhb•SOHRB], water and nutrients from the soil. **Nutrients** [NOO•tree•uhntz] are materials that living things such as plants need to grow.

Some roots are long and can reach water deep under the ground. Some roots have many small, hairy branches that spread out just under the soil to get water from a large area. Water and nutrients move from the roots to other parts of the plant.

A plant's roots absorb water and nutrients from the soil.

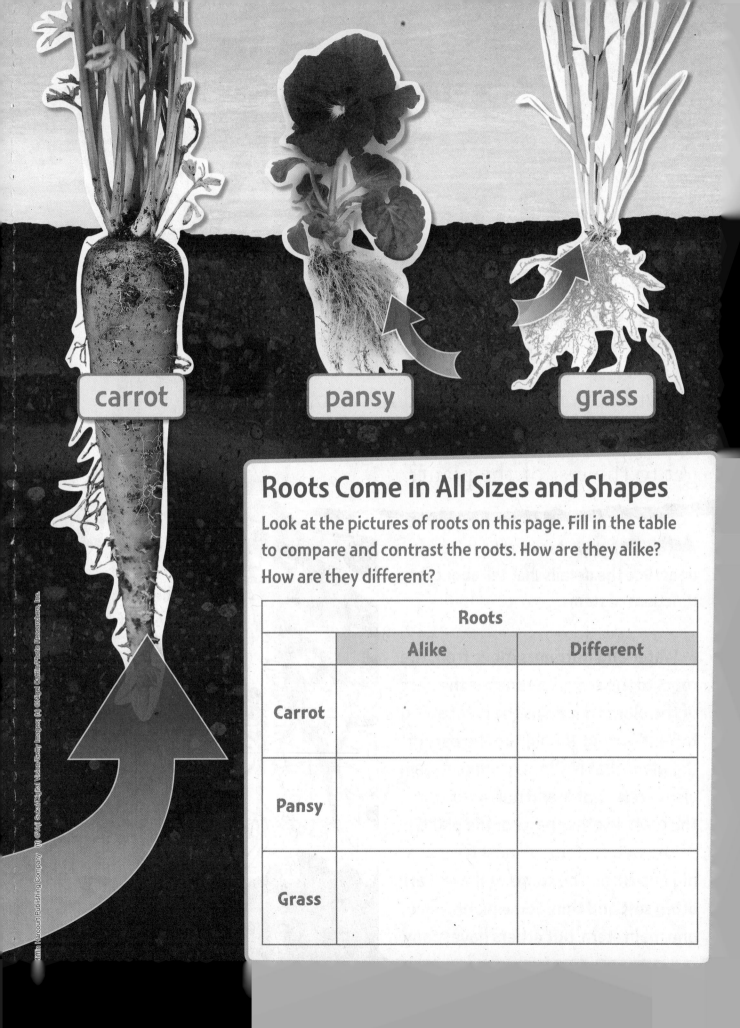

carrot

pansy

grass

Roots Come in All Sizes and Shapes

Look at the pictures of roots on this page. Fill in the table to compare and contrast the roots. How are they alike? How are they different?

	Roots	
	Alike	**Different**
Carrot		
Pansy		
Grass		

Reach for the Sky

What happens to water and nutrients after they enter the roots? How do they get to the rest of the plant?

oak tree

A plant's stem carries water and nutrients from the roots to the rest of the plant.

As you read this page, underline the details that tell about the functions of stems.

Water and nutrients move from the roots to the stem. The stem is the part of the plant that helps the plant stand tall and strong. It holds up the part of the plant that is above ground. A stem also carries water and nutrients from the roots to other parts of the plant.

The woody stems of most trees are big and thick. The stems of flowers are often soft and thin. Some plants have one main stem, but others have many.

passion vine

yellow daisy

Do the Math!
Make a Graph

Use the data to create a bar graph to compare the lengths of different plant stems.

Type of Plant	Length of Stem
Dogwood tree	650 cm
Bamboo	400 cm
Broccoli	50 cm
Saw palmetto	200 cm

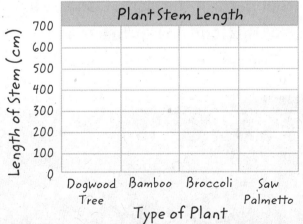

Plant Stem Length

Length of Stem (cm)

700
600
500
400
300
200
100
0

Dogwood Tree   Bamboo   Broccoli   Saw Palmetto

Type of Plant

Plant Food!

Water and nutrients keep a plant healthy. But a plant still needs food to survive. Luckily, a plant doesn't need to go anywhere to get its food!

Active Reading As you read these pages, draw one line under a cause. Draw two lines under an effect.

Unlike animals, most plants can make their own food. This important process takes place in leaves.

Leaves use water, air, and light energy from the sun to make food. The food is then transported from the leaves through the plant's stems to other parts of the plant. Plants use most of this food energy to live and grow. The rest of the food is stored.

sunflower

Leaves use water, air, and sunlight to make food. Food made in leaves is transported to the rest of the plant.

palm tree

Leaves are many different sizes and shapes. Look at the picture of the sunflower plant. Its leaves are big and wide. Big, wide leaves can catch more sunlight. This helps the plant make more food.

bush

Show the Flow

Draw a plant growing in soil. Draw different-colored arrows to show how water, nutrients, and food move in different directions through the plant.

The Cycle of Life

The tallest tree in the world was once small enough to fit in your hand. Like you, plants start out small and grow bigger.

Active Reading As you read this page, write numbers next to the appropriate sentences to show the order of steps in the reproduction of an apple tree.

The blossoms on apple trees and other plants are called flowers. A **flower** is the plant part that helps some plants reproduce [ree•pruh•DOOS]. When living things **reproduce**, they make new living things like themselves.

First, flowers grow into fruit. After the fruit ripens, it falls to the ground. The fruit contains seeds. A **seed** has a small plant inside of it. A seed also has food for the small plant.

Then sunlight, soil, water, and air help the seeds sprout into seedlings and grow. The seedlings grow into adult plants. The life cycle continues as the adult plants produce more flowers and seeds.

© Houghton Mifflin Harcourt Publishing Company   HMH Credits (tree) ©Frank Krahmer/Photographer's Choice RF/Getty Images

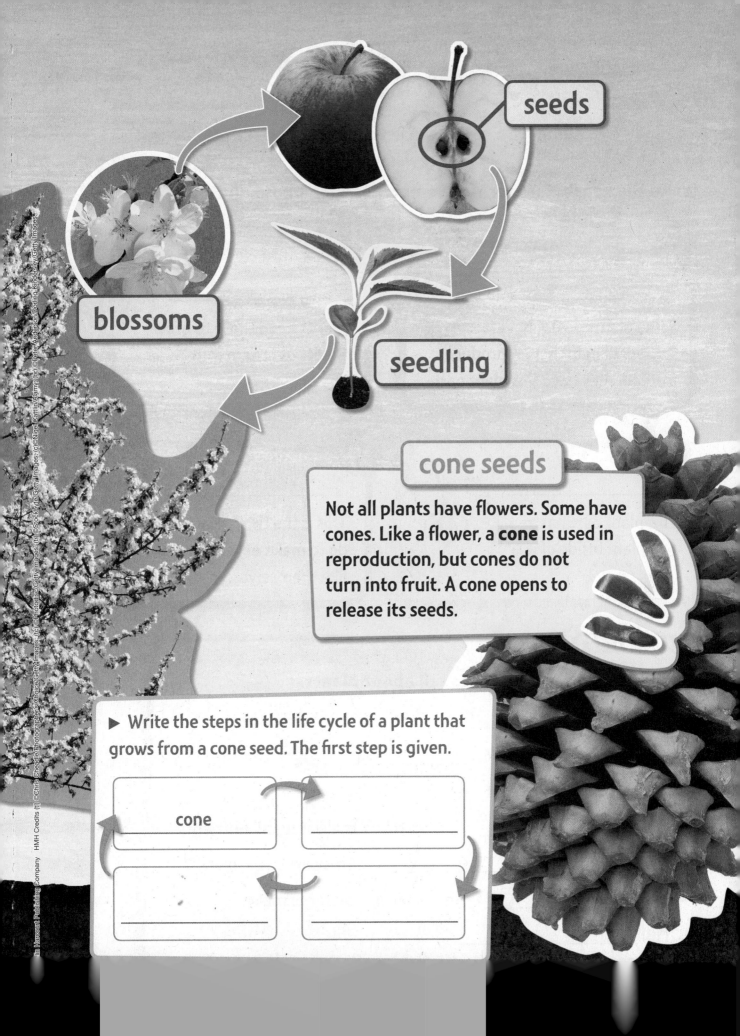

seeds

blossoms

seedling

cone seeds

Not all plants have flowers. Some have cones. Like a flower, a **cone** is used in reproduction, but cones do not turn into fruit. A cone opens to release its seeds.

▶ Write the steps in the life cycle of a plant that grows from a cone seed. The first step is given.

cone _____

_____

_____

_____

Sum It Up!

When you're done, use the answer key to check and revise your work.

Write the vocabulary term that matches each photo and caption.

1
_____

Some plants do not have flowers to help them reproduce. Instead, they have this plant part.

2
_____

Plants need these to grow. Plants get them from the soil.

3
_____

This plant part has a tiny plant inside of it.

4
_____

This is the thing plants do to make new plants like themselves.

Summarize

Fill in the missing words to tell about plants.

The (5) _____ of the plant absorb water

and nutrients from the (6) _____. The

water and nutrients next move from the roots to the

(7) _____. From there, the water and nutrients

move to the (8) _____. This part of the plant

uses (9) _____, air, and water to make

(10) _____.

Answer Key: 1. cone 2. nutrients 3. seed 4. reproduce 5. roots 6. soil
7. stem 8. leaves 9. sunlight 10. food

Name _____

Word Play

1 Use the words in the box to identify the parts of a plant. Tell one function of each part.

| roots | stem | leaf | flower* | *Key Lesson Vocabulary |

_____

_____

_____

_____

_____

_____

_____

_____

_____

_____

_____

_____

Apply Concepts

2 Draw the life cycle of a peach tree. The first stage is already done.

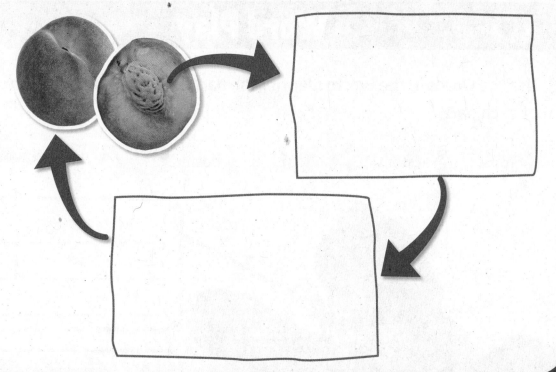

Find two different types of plants near your school.

3 How are these plants different?

_____

4 How are these plants similar?

_____

5 Which parts of the two plants can you see?

_____

Take It Home!

Work with a family member to grow a plant you can eat. When the plant is fully grown, discuss its different parts and how they help the plant. Then share it with your family as a snack!

SC.3.L.14.1 Describe structures in plants and their roles in food production, support, water and nutrient transport, and reproduction.

People in Science

5 Things to Know About Rosa Ortiz

1 Rosa Ortiz is a botanist. She studies plants.

2 Ortiz studies a family of plants called the moonseed family.

3 Moonseed is a woody vine. It has poisonous parts.

4 Ortiz travels to many places to study moonseed.

5 The roots of some types of moonseed have been used as medicine.

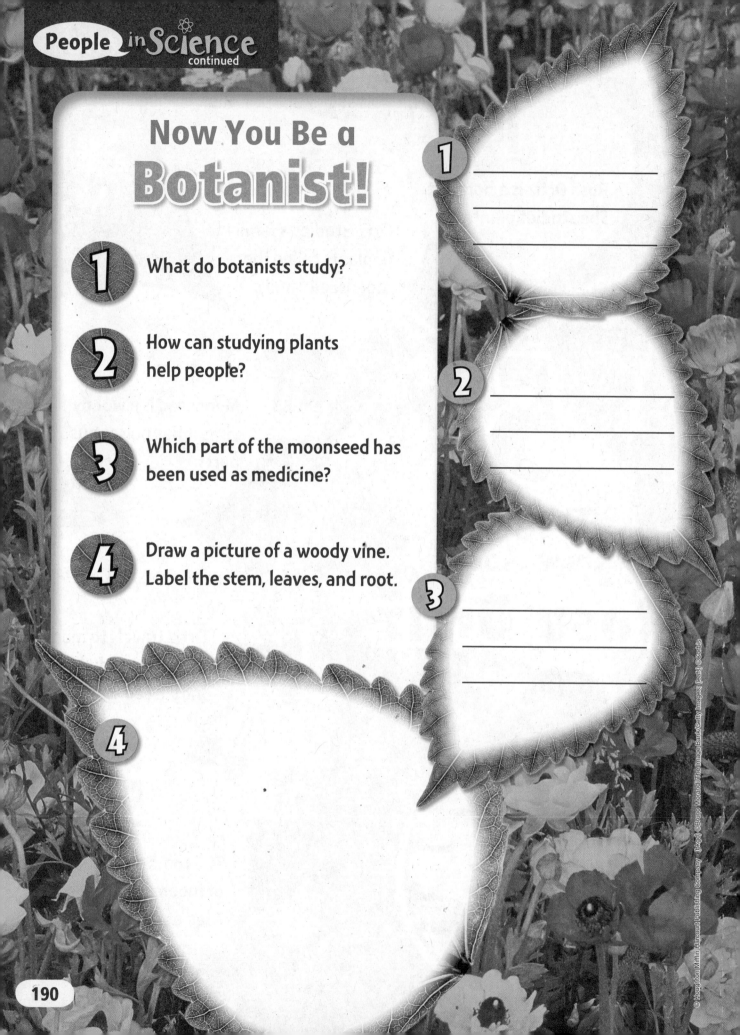

Now You Be a Botanist!

1 What do botanists study?

2 How can studying plants help people?

3 Which part of the moonseed has been used as medicine?

4 Draw a picture of a woody vine. Label the stem, leaves, and root.

1 _____

_____

_____

2 _____

_____

_____

3 _____

_____

_____

SC.3.N.1.3 Keep records as appropriate...
SC.3.N.1.4 Recognize the importance of communication among scientists.
SC.3.N.1.5 Recognize that scientists question, discuss, and check each others' evidence and explanations. **SC.3.N.1.6** Infer based on observation. **SC.3.L.14.2** Investigate and describe how plants respond to stimuli (heat, light, gravity), such as the way plant stems grow toward light and their roots grow downward in response to gravity.

Name _____

Essential Question

How Do Plants Respond to Light?

Set a Purpose
In this investigation, you will share your results with other groups. Why do you think scientists share their results?

_____

_____

_____

_____

Think About the Procedure
Why does each group face the opening in its shoebox in a different direction?

_____

_____

_____

Predict what will happen to the seedlings.

_____

_____

_____

_____

_____

Record Your Data
In the space below, draw how the seedlings responded to light.

Draw Conclusions

What did you observe? Infer why the seedlings responded as they did.

_____

_____

_____

_____

_____

_____

Analyze and Extend

1. Compare your observations with those of other groups. Did all groups have the same results? Why or why not?

_____

_____

_____

_____

_____

2. Plants respond to temperature as well as light. How could you design an experiment to find out how temperature affects plants?

_____

_____

_____

_____

_____

_____

_____

3. Think of other questions you would like to ask about the way plants grow.

_____

_____

_____

_____

_____

SC.3.N.1.6 Infer based on observation. **SC.3.L.14.2** Investigate and describe how plants respond to stimuli (heat, light, gravity), such as the way plant stems grow toward light and their roots grow downward in response to gravity.

Essential Question

How Do Plants Respond to Their Environment?

Engage Your Brain!

Find the answer to the following question in this lesson and record it here.

This tree fell over and then began growing upward again. Why?

_____

_____

_____

Active Reading

Lesson Vocabulary
List the terms. As you learn about each one, makes notes in the Interactive Glossary.

_____

_____

Main Idea and Details
Detail sentences give information about a topic. The information may be examples, features, characteristics, or facts. Active readers stay focused on the topic when they ask, What fact or information does this sentence add to the topic?

Plants and Light

What happens when you go from a dark room into a bright room? You blink! Blinking is a response to light. Plants respond to light, too.

Active Reading As you read these two pages, draw two lines under each main idea.

Hi. My name is Maria. I like learning about plants. One day, I put my plant in a dark room with one window. A week later, it looked like this! The plant began growing toward the light.

Growing toward light is one way that plants respond to their environment. The **environment** is all the living and nonliving things in a place. Growing toward light helps plants make more food.

© Houghton Mifflin Harcourt Publishing Company (b) ©Cathy Melloan/Alamy

Morning glory flowers open in the morning sun and last only one day.

By afternoon, the flowers close up and die.

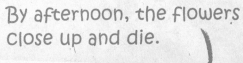

Flowering plants respond to light in more than one way. The flowers of some plants open during the day and close at night. Other plants have flowers that open at night and close during the day. The bright yellow flowers of the sunflower plant face the sun throughout the day. The flowers move from east to west, following the sun as it crosses the sky.

What Will the Plant Do?

Look at the picture of the plant on the opposite page. Imagine that you turned the plant around so that it was growing away from the light. Explain and draw what would happen to the plant.

_____

_____

The Heat Is On!

What happens when it gets very warm out? You sweat! Sweating is a response to the rising temperature. Plants respond to rising temperatures, too.

Active Reading As you read these pages, circle the sentences that explain how plants respond to a change in temperature.

In the winter, the branches of a tree in my grandmother's yard were bare. In spring, the temperature changed, and the weather got warmer. The tree was covered with buds!

This tree gets buds in the spring.

Hyacinth bulbs must go through a period of cooler weather before they will grow again in the warmer temperatures of springtime.

Leaf budding is one way that plants respond to heat. The buds come out when the temperature warms. The buds change into leaves.

How else do plants respond to temperature changes? Temperature affects when seeds germinate. **Germinate** [JER•muh•nayt] means that the seeds start to grow.

You might notice that when the temperature is warmer in spring, seedlings begin to grow. For example, acorns begin to grow into oak trees.

Some plants will not release their seeds unless it is burning hot! Some pinecones only open and release their seeds after a forest fire.

Some cones release their seeds in response to fire.

What's the Effect?

Fill in the chart below to show details about plants and heat.

> Plants respond to temperature.

© Houghton Mifflin Harcourt Publishing Company   (bl) ©Dan Suzio/Photo Researchers, Inc.; (tc) ©John Block/Botanica/Getty Images; (tr) ©Dave King/Dorling Kindersley/Getty Images.

Cold Snap

What happens when it's really cold outside? Your teeth chatter! Plants respond to cold weather, too.

In late fall, the oranges on our orange tree were ready to pick. Before we could pick them, the weather got really cold. There was a freeze. The fruit was ruined!

Weather below 0 °C, or a *freeze*, can harm a plant. Sometimes the freeze happens when the plant is flowering. The flowers die. The plant will not produce fruit. Sometimes the freeze happens when the fruit is on the tree. As Maria said, the fruit is ruined!

A freeze damaged these trees and fruit.

Cold weather has not damaged these oranges. They are ready to pick.

There are ways to keep plants safe from freezes. People can spray the fruit with water. Ice forms over the fruit and protects it from the cold!

Do the Math!
Interpret a Graph

The graph shows the number of ripe oranges picked from Maria's tree for five years. Study the graph and then answer the questions.

Number of Oranges on Maria's Tree

Year	Oranges
2006	🍊🍊🍊🍊🍊🍊
2007	🍊🍊🍊🍊
2008	🍊🍊
2009	🍊🍊🍊🍊
2010	🍊🍊🍊🍊🍊🍊🍊🍊🍊🍊

Key: Each 🍊 = 10 oranges

1. How many oranges were picked each year?

_____

_____

_____

_____

2. In which years do you think a freeze occurred? Why?

_____

_____

_____

Up or Down?

What happens when you jump? Gravity pulls you back. Plants respond to gravity, too.

Active Reading As you read this page, find and underline details about a plant responding to gravity.

Gravity pulls things toward Earth's center. A plant's roots respond to gravity by growing mostly downward. A plant's stem responds in the opposite way. The stem grows upward, away from the pull of gravity. Even when a plant gets tipped on its side, the plant's stem will slowly start to grow upward again.

Stems grow up.

Roots grow down.

Growing against the pull of gravity gave this tree a bend in its trunk.

I know that gravity makes plant roots grow downward and stems grow upward. So what would happen if I turned a bean plant on its side?

①

The stem of this bean plant grows upward, away from gravity.

②

On its side, the bean plant's stem continues to grow opposite the pull of gravity.

▶ Predict what the plant will do if the pot is turned upright again.

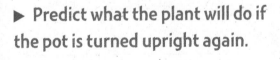

_____

▶ Draw what the plant will look like after a few weeks.

③

Sum It Up!

When you're done, use the answer key to check
and revise your work.

Complete the graphic organizer using details from the summary below.

Plants respond to their environment.
They grow toward light. Plant leaves
bud and seeds germinate when the
temperature is right. Their roots and
stems grow in certain directions in
response to the pull of gravity.

1

Detail: _____

_____

_____

**Main Idea: Plants respond
to their environment.**

2

Detail: _____

_____

_____

3

Detail: _____

_____

_____

_____

Answer Key: 1. Plants grow toward light. 2. Plant
leaves bud and seeds germinate when the
temperature is right. 3. Plant roots and stems grow
in certain directions in response to gravity.

Name _____

Word Play

1 Use the clues and the words in the box to complete the puzzle.

Across

2. Some pine cones open only when this is very high.

4. Forming flowers or leaves

Down

1. This pulls things toward Earth's center

3. All the living and nonliving things around a living thing

5. Begin to grow

budding   environment*   germinate*   gravity   temperature

*Key Lesson Vocabulary

Apply Concepts

2 Draw an arrow from the cause to the effect.

3 In the image above, what is the cone doing in response to heat?

_____

4 Draw arrows to show which direction roots and stems will grow in response to gravity.

5 What is happening in the picture?

_____

_____

_____

Take It Home! Share what you have learned about plant responses with your family. Explain how a plant responds to light, temperature, and gravity.

Benchmark Review

Name _____

Multiple Choice

Identify the choice that best answers the question.

SC.3.L.14.2

1 A class was divided into small groups to do experiments with plants and light. Each group used the same kind of plants. The chart below shows the data from two of the groups.

Plant number	Location	Bending toward light?
Group 1		
1	outside	no
2	inside by window	yes
3	inside in dark corner	yes
Group 2		
1	outside	no
2	inside by window	yes
3	inside in dark closet	no

Which explains why one of the inside plants did **not** bend toward the light?

(A) Some plants do not need light.

(B) Inside plants usually do not bend toward light.

(C) The plant in the corner did not get enough fresh air.

(D) If a plant does not sense light, it won't bend toward that light.

SC.3.L.14.1

2 Martin puts a seedling plant in a glass of water. He knows the plant will absorb the water. In what order will the water travel through the parts of the plant?

(F) leaves, roots, stem

(G) roots, leaves, stem

(H) roots, stem, leaves

(I) stem, leaves, roots

SC.3.L.14.1

3 Look at the diagram of the plant below.

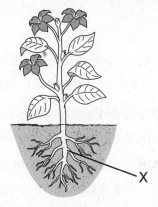

What is a function of the part of the plant labeled X?

(A) to hold the plant in the ground

(B) to make food for the plant

(C) to help the plant reproduce

(D) to transport water to the leaves

SC.3.L.14.1, SC.3.N.3.2

4 Kiara makes a model of an apple tree. She includes leaves, roots, and stems. Which part is missing?

(F) seeds

(G) flowers

(H) cones

(I) acorns

SC.3.L.14.1

5 Joella places Plant A and Plant B in a sunny spot. They are the same type of plant and put in the same type of soil. She waters Plant A every other day and Plant B only once a week. After two weeks, the plants look like this.

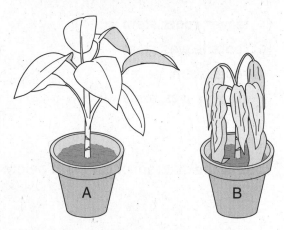

Which statement **best** explains what Joella can conclude about Plant B?

Ⓐ Plant B did not get any food.

Ⓑ Plant B did not get any nutrients.

Ⓒ Plant B did not get enough water.

Ⓓ Plant B did not get enough sunlight.

SC.3.L.14.2, SC.3.N.3.3

6 Crystal is making a model of a pine cone. How will her model be different from a real pine cone?

Ⓕ Her model will not be the same size.

Ⓖ Her model will not open after a fire.

Ⓗ Her model will not be the same color.

Ⓘ Her model will not be the same shape.

SC.3.L.14.1, SC.3.N.1.6

7 Katrina observes the plant part shown here with a hand lens.

Which statement **best** describes what Katrina can write in her science notebook about this plant part?

Ⓐ It is the part that gets water from the ground.

Ⓑ It is the part of the plant in which food is made.

Ⓒ It is the part of the plant that will bloom into a flower.

Ⓓ It contains a small plant that can grow into a larger plant.

SC.3.L.14.1

8 Food is made in the leaves of plants. Which answer **best** explains the pathway of food through the plant?

Ⓕ leaves to stems to roots

Ⓖ leaves to flowers to roots

Ⓗ leaves to roots to flowers

Ⓘ leaves to flowers to stems

SC.3.L.14.1

9 Jamal notices that there are needle-like leaves on a tree in his back yard. Which one of the following **best** describes what the needles do for the plant?

Ⓐ support the plant

Ⓑ make food for the plant

Ⓒ transport water to the roots

Ⓓ produce seeds for the plant to reproduce

SC.3.L.14.1

10 Carlos has drawn this picture of a plant he is studying. He labels one part of the plant and marks it A.

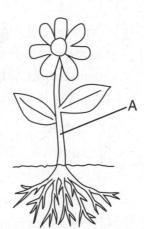

What caption should Carlos write next to the letter A?

(F) Makes food

(G) Absorbs water

(H) Anchors the plant

(I) Carries nutrients

SC.3.L.14.2, SC.3.N.1.5

11 Andrea uses three different plants to show that stems grow against gravity. She shows other scientists her evidence. What should the scientists do?

(A) check her evidence

(B) give her an award

(C) tell her that her conclusion is wrong

(D) tell her she did not use enough plants

SC.3.L.14.1

12 Mohammad draws a diagram of a flowering plant in his science notebook. He draws a line next to a leaf on the plant. Which of the following would be the **best** label for this part of the plant?

(F) Makes food

(G) Absorbs water

(H) Attracts insects

(I) Transports water

SC.3.L.14.2

13 Jorge places his plant by a light. The picture shows the plant and the light.

What would happen if Jorge placed the light on the other side of the plant?

(A) The leaves would die.

(B) The flower would close.

(C) The root would grow upward.

(D) The stem would grow toward the light.

SC.3.L.14.1, SC.3.N.1.6

14 Study the plant parts in the picture.

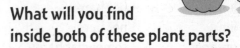

What will you find inside both of these plant parts?

(F) seeds   (H) tiny leaves

(G) flowers   (I) tiny plants

SC.3.L.14.2, SC.3.N.1.4

15 Rex and Lily study plants. Rex's data tells him that plant roots store food. Lily's data tells her that plants make food in their leaves. Why is it important for them to share their data?

(A) to prove roots make food

(B) to check each other's evidence

(C) to learn how flowers help the plant

(D) to prove that stems transport water

SC.3.L.14.2

16 Leaves are the plant's food factories. They use water, air, and sunlight to make food. Which of the following responses helps a plant to make food?

(F) The roots grow toward light.

(G) The stems grow toward light.

(H) The flowers grow downward to resist gravity.

(I) The leaves grow upward in response to gravity.

SC.3.L.14.2

17 Some tree blossoms are hardy. That means they can survive a bad frost. Other tree blossoms are not hardy. They are easily hurt by frost. The table below shows the hardiness of different tree blossoms.

Tree blossom	Hardiness
grapefruit	somewhat hardy
lemon	not hardy
lime	not hardy
orange	somewhat hardy
mandarin	hardy

Which of the following tree blossoms would be **least likely** to survive a frost?

(A) lime and lemon

(B) lemon and grapefruit

(C) orange and mandarin

(D) grapefruit and orange

SC.3.L.14.2

18 Some wheat plants need to go through a period of cold temperatures to grow into adult plants. When would be the **best** time to plant these wheat seeds?

(F) spring   (H) fall

(G) summer   (I) winter

SC.3.L.14.2

19 Florida is known for its year-round mild weather, but one spring the temperatures did not rise above 21 °C. The table below shows the temperatures at which different plants bud.

Plant	Budding temperatures (°C)
1	13 to 15
2	17 to 20
3	23 to 25
4	23 to 26
5	24 to 26

Which of the plants were able to bud?

(A) plants 1 and 2   (C) plants 3 and 4

(B) plants 2 and 3   (D) plants 4 and 5

SC.3.L.14.2, SC.3.N.1.3

20 Denise's test shows that plants grow toward light. She wants to show others what she observed. How can she best record her results?

(F) draw a picture

(G) make a bar graph

(H) write a paragraph

(I) make a data table

Classifying Plants and Animals

Houghton Mifflin Harcourt Publishing Company   (border) ©INDisc/Age Fotostock; (okad) ©Inga Spence/Photo Researchers, Inc.; (inset) ©Douglas Faulkner/Photo Researchers, Inc.

Big Idea 15

Diversity and Evolution of Living Organisms

Blue Spring State Park, Orange City, Florida

I Wonder Why

A manatee is sometimes called a sea cow. Why might a manatee be called a cow? *Turn the page to find out.*

Here's Why Manatees and cows are alike in a few ways. Both are vertebrates and both are mammals.

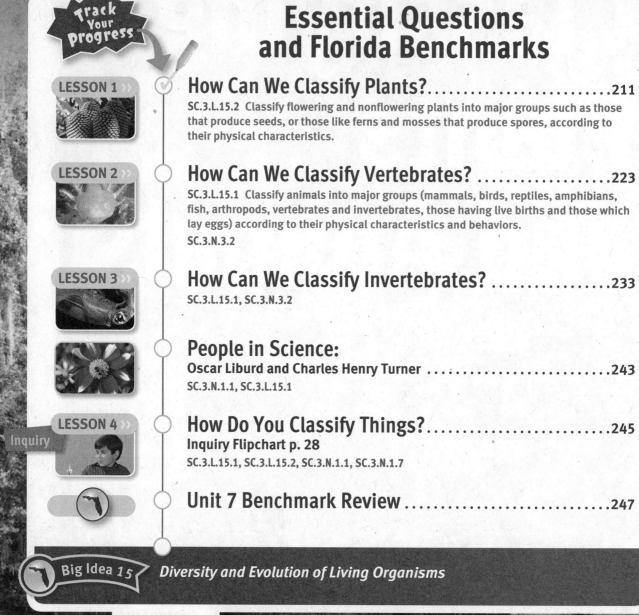

Track Your Progress

Essential Questions and Florida Benchmarks

Big Idea 15 *Diversity and Evolution of Living Organisms*

Now I Get the Big Idea!

SC.3.L.15.2 Classify flowering and non-flowering plants into major groups such as those that produce seeds, or those like ferns and mosses that produce spores, according to their physical characteristics.

Lesson **1**

Essential Question

How Can We Classify Plants?

Engage Your Brain!

Find the answer to the following question in this lesson and record it here.

The sticky parts of the sundew plant catch insects. How is this sundew like an orchid?

_____

_____

Active Reading

Lesson Vocabulary

List each term. As you learn about each one, make notes in the Interactive Glossary.

_____

_____

_____

Visual Aids

A photo adds information to the text that appears on the page with it. Active readers pause their reading to review the photos and decide how the information in them adds to what is provided in the text.

211

Sorting Plants

There are so many plants! How can you classify, or group, them? Let's find out.

Active Reading As you read these two pages, draw circles around two words that are key to understanding the main idea.

One way to classify plants is to group them by their type. For example, think about how all trees are the same or how all shrubs are the same.

Another way to classify plants is to look at their parts. You can group plants that have similar leaves, stems, or roots.

vine

Kinds of Plants

There are many kinds of plants. Vines, trees, and shrubs are three kinds of plants. Vines have long, thin stems. Trees are woody plants that grow tall. Trees have one main stem. Shrubs are similar to trees, but smaller and with many stems.

tree

shrub

pine needle

palm leaf

Plant Parts

One plant part you can use to classify a plant is its leaves. Look at their shape, color, and size. Pine needles are long, thin, and green. Maple leaves have many points. They can be many different shades of green. Palm leaves are very large and fan-shaped or feather-like.

maple leaf

How to Group?

How else can you classify plants?

_____

Draw two plants that you can classify this way.

Blooming!

Roses, tulips, daisies—how are they the same? Read on to find out.

Active Reading As you read these two pages, draw circles around the names of flowering plants.

Plants that make flowers are classified as **flowering plants**. Flowering plants are the largest plant group. They are found in deserts, rain forests, and even under water. The flowers of plants have many sizes, colors, and shapes. Let's look at some!

► Circle yes or no to classify these plants.

Does it make flowers?

yes   no

Does it make seeds?

yes   no

Orchids are the largest family of flowering plants.

The corpse flower is the largest flower of all. It can weigh more than 20 pounds!

Some hibiscus plants grow flowers all year long.

Seeds

Flowers may look pretty, but they have a job to do. They make fruits with seeds. Oranges and strawberries are examples of fruits with seeds. Each seed has a new plant inside it.

Some magnolia trees grow large, pink flowers.

Do the Math!
Use Patterns

Write the number of petals on each flower. Then draw a flower that could complete each pattern.

Cones!

Not all plants make flowers. Some plants make seeds in other ways.

Active Reading As you read this page, draw a star next to what you think is the most important sentence. Be ready to explain why.

Non-flowering plants are plants that do not make flowers. Even though they do not make flowers, many non-flowering plants make seeds. Pine trees are non-flowering plants. Their seeds develop inside cones. Take a look at other plants that make seeds in cones.

▶ Circle yes or no to classify these plants.

Does it make flowers?	yes	no
Does it make seeds?	yes	no

Sequoia [si•KWOY•uh] trees grow very tall, but they make small cones!

Joint firs grow in dry places. They make small red cones.

Plant Riddle

Read the riddle, then write the answer.

I am very tall.
I grow small cones compared to my size.
What am I?

_____

These eastern cape cycads [sy•kadz] make cones like the ones shown above.

Even More!

Plants with flowers make seeds.
Plants with cones make seeds.
Do all plants make seeds? Find out.

Active Reading As you read these two pages, draw a line from each picture to one sentence that describes it.

Mosses and ferns are also non-flowering plants. Mosses are small, soft plants. They often grow together in groups. Ferns are larger plants with leaves called fronds.

Mosses and ferns do not make flowers, cones, or seeds. They make spores. Like seeds, **spores** are plant parts that can grow into new plants.

Mosses can grow on rocks and trees. Mosses do not grow tall. This "green carpet" is actually made up of many tiny moss plants.

Ferns have leaves called fronds. Each leaf has smaller leaflets that branch off from the stem.

Spores

Spores are released from the stalks of this moss. In ferns, spores form in small groups on the underside of the fronds. Each group contains hundreds of spores.

moss

fern

This staghorn fern grows on trees.

▶ Read each statement. Circle T if the statement is true and F if it is false.

1. Spores are seeds.	T	F
2. Spores are found in cones.	T	F
3. Mosses do not make flowers.	T	F
4. Ferns make flowers.	T	F
5. Mosses do not make seeds.	T	F

Sum It Up!

When you're done, use the answer key to check and revise your work.

The idea web below summarizes the lesson. Give two examples of each type of plant described below.

1

Kinds of Plants

Plants can be sorted into many types.

_____

_____

2

Flowering Plants

This is the largest group of plants. Flowers make seeds.

_____

_____

Main Idea

There are many ways to classify plants.

3

Non-flowering Plants with Cones

Plants with cones do not make flowers, but they do make seeds. Seeds form inside the cones.

_____

_____

4

Non-flowering Plants with Spores

Some plants make spores but do not make seeds. Spores make new plants.

_____

_____

Answer Key: 1. vines, shrubs, trees 2. magnolias, orchids, corpse flowers, or hibiscus 3. pines, sequoias, joint firs, or cycads 4. ferns and mosses

© Houghton Mifflin Harcourt Publishing Company   (tr) ©Photodisc/Getty Images; (bl) ©Peter Anderson/Dorling Kindersley/Getty Images; (br) ©Gusto/Photo Researchers, Inc.

 **Brain Check**

Name _____

Word Play

1 Read the clues. Unscramble the letters to complete the clue.

1. When you group something, you
   _____ it.   y s l i c f s a

2. Some plants make tiny _____   p r o s s e
   instead of seeds.

3. _____ grow on some non-flowering   c s e o n
   plants and hold new seeds inside them.

4. Plants with _____, such as roses   r o w e l f s
   and daisies, are the largest group of plants.

5. _____ plants are small non-flowering   s m o s
   plants that grow from spores.

6. _____ have special leaves called   f r e s n
   fronds.

Apply Concepts

2 Write the letter of the correct description under each picture.

a. I grow seeds and make flowers. Who am I?

b. I grow seeds, but they form in cones. Who am I?

c. I don't grow flowers or seeds. Who am I?

_____   _____   _____

3 Suppose scientists find a new kind of plant in a rain forest. What are three questions they might ask to help them classify the plant?

_____

_____

_____

_____

_____

_____

Take It Home!

Have each family member write *flowering plants* and *non-flowering plants* on paper. List as many of each type of plant as you can. Share lists. Get a point for each plant no one else lists.

SC.3.L.15.1 Classify animals into major groups (mammals, birds, reptiles, amphibians, fish, arthropods, vertebrates and invertebrates, those having live births and those which lay eggs) according to their physical characteristics and behaviors.

Lesson 2

Essential Question

How Can We Classify Vertebrates?

Engage Your Brain!

Find the answer to the following question in this lesson and record it here.

How would you classify this animal?

_____

_____

_____

Active Reading

Lesson Vocabulary

List each term. As you learn about each one, make notes in the Interactive Glossary.

_____

_____

_____

Signal Words: Comparison

Signal words show connections between ideas. Words that signal comparisons, or similarities, include *like, alike, same as, similar to,* and *resembles.* Active readers remember what they read because they are alert to signal words that identify comparisons.

Have a Backbone!

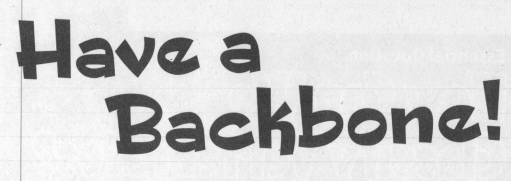

Some boas live in thick forests. Their backbones let them curl up and stretch out!

What do you have in common with fish, alligators, frogs, birds, and seals? Why, it's your backbone!

Active Reading As you read these two pages, find and underline the definition of *vertebrate*.

Animals that have a backbone are called **vertebrates**. There are many kinds of vertebrates. Frogs, birds, snakes, and tigers are all vertebrates. Vertebrates live in many places.

Lions live in grasslands. Their young are called cubs.

Fish

Fish are vertebrates, too. Fish are many sizes, shapes, and colors. Some fish are tiny. Other fish, such as the whale shark, are large. A whale shark can grow as long as a school bus! Fish take in oxygen through their gills and spend their whole lives in water.

Sea Horse

Male sea horses carry eggs in a part of their body called a pouch.

Monkfish

This fish lives deep in the ocean where there is no light.

Bass

This bass lives in fresh water. Like most kinds of fish, it lays eggs.

Do the Math!

Measure in Centimeters

Alexa's goby is about 3 centimeters long. Draw a fish this long.

Samuel's goldfish is 6 centimeters long. Draw a fish this long.

Amphibian or Reptile?

How are amphibians and reptiles different? Read on to learn about these two groups.

Active Reading As you read these two pages, draw circles around the clue words that signal when things are being compared.

Frog

This amphibian lives around water.

Turtle

This reptile lays eggs.

Amphibians [am•FIB•ee•uhnz] start life in water. Many amphibians move to land as they grow. Salamanders, toads, and frogs are amphibians. Like most other amphibians, frogs lay their eggs in water. When the eggs hatch, the tadpoles look like fish. Most amphibians have smooth, moist skin. Young amphibians have gills. Many adult amphibians have lungs.

Reptiles are animals with scales covering their bodies. Lizards and turtles are reptiles. Similar to amphibians, most reptiles hatch from eggs. A reptile breathes with lungs its whole life. Reptiles, such as crocodiles, that spend a lot of time in water must come up for air.

Identify

▶ Read the facts on each trading card. In the circles, write an "A" for amphibian or an "R" for reptile. Then color the borders green for reptiles or orange for amphibians.

Alligator

Alligators are covered with large scales. They lay eggs in nests.

Newt

Newts lay their eggs in water.

Gecko

Geckos are covered with scales. They breathe using lungs.

Mudpuppy

Mudpuppies have smooth, moist skin.

Frilled Lizard

R

Frilled lizards lay their eggs on the ground.

Salamander

A

Birds and Mammals

What are some other vertebrate groups? Read to find out.

Active Reading As you read these two pages, underline three characteristics of birds and circle three characteristics of mammals.

Birds are another kind of vertebrate. Birds are animals that have wings, feathers, and beaks and lay eggs. Some birds, such as the hummingbird, are tiny. Other birds, such as the ostrich, are very large. Birds breathe with lungs.

Owl B

Penguin B

Penguins have wings, but they cannot fly.

Flamingo B

Flamingos live in places with shallow water.

Bee-eater B

Bee-eaters have colorful feathers.

Golden Pheasant B

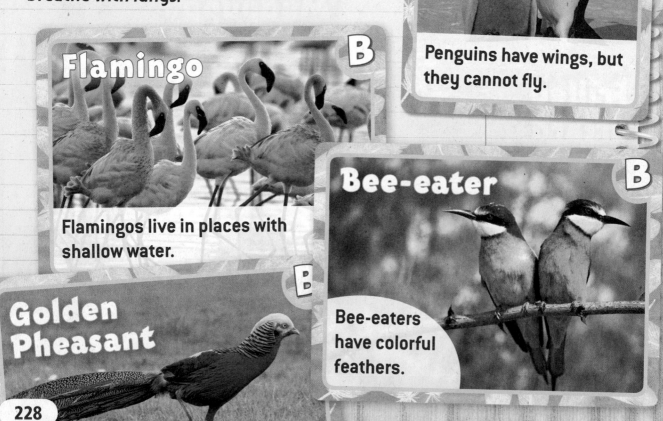

Elephants, apes, whales, and dolphins are all mammals. How are they alike? **Mammals** are animals that have fur or hair. Most do not lay eggs. Instead, female mammals give birth to live young and make milk to feed them. Mammals also use lungs to breathe.

Squirrel M

Bearded Seal M

Can you tell why this animal is called a bearded seal?

Kangaroo M

When a kangaroo is born, it crawls into its mother's pouch.

Emperor Tamarin M M

This monkey has hair covering its body.

▶ Draw your own bird or mammal card. Label its characteristics.

Black Bear M

Sum It Up!

When you're done, use the answer key to check and revise your work.

Write the animal type on the line and then draw a line to the matching picture.

1 A _____ has fur or hair covering its body and gives birth to live young.

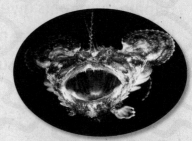

2 A _____ lives in water and takes in oxygen through gills.

3 A _____ lives on land or in water and has scales.

4 A _____ has feathers and wings.

5 An _____ has moist skin and begins life in the water.

Brain Check

Name _____

Word Play

1 Complete the maze to connect each animal to its classification at the bottom. Pass through each animal's traits along the way.

goldfish   salamander   snake   hippo   owl

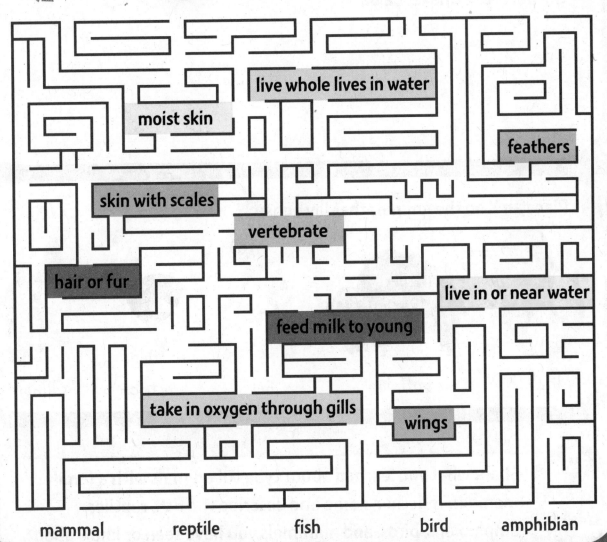

live whole lives in water

moist skin

feathers

skin with scales

vertebrate

hair or fur

live in or near water

feed milk to young

take in oxygen through gills

wings

mammal   reptile   fish   bird   amphibian

Apply Concepts

2 You are hiking along a river. You see an animal that looks like it could be either a lizard or a salamander. What are questions you could ask the guide to help you decide which animal it is?

_____

_____

_____

3 Draw an imaginary bird. Label the parts that make it a bird.

4 Place an X on the animals that lay eggs.

lizard   buffalo   newt   ostrich   salmon

Share what you learned about types of animals with a family member. Together, name and describe the fish, reptiles, amphibians, birds, and mammals you have seen or know about.

SC.3.N.3.2 Recognize that scientists use models to help understand and explain how things work. SC.3.L.15.1 Classify animals into major groups (mammals, birds, reptiles, amphibians, fish, arthropods, vertebrates and invertebrates, those having live births and those which lay eggs) according to their physical characteristics and behaviors.

Essential Question

How Can We Classify Invertebrates?

Engage Your Brain!

Find the answer to the following question in this lesson and record it here.

Look at this "furry lobster." How do you know it is not a mammal?

_____

_____

_____

_____

Active Reading

Lesson Vocabulary

List each term. As you learn about each one, make notes in the Interactive Glossary.

_____

_____

Main Idea and Details

Detail sentences give information about a topic. The information may be examples, features, characteristics, or facts. Active readers stay focused on the topic when they ask, What fact or information does this sentence add to the topic?

No Bones!

How are an octopus, lobster, cricket, and worm alike? They are all invertebrates.

Active Reading As you read these two pages, find and underline lesson vocabulary each time it is used.

Invertebrates are animals without backbones. There are many kinds of invertebrates. Jellyfish, crabs, spiders, worms, and insects are some kinds. Invertebrates live in many places, from the ocean to your own backyard.

A worm has no backbone or hard outer covering.

Most kinds of female sea stars release tiny eggs from each of their arms into ocean water.

The snail has a hard shell to protect its soft body.

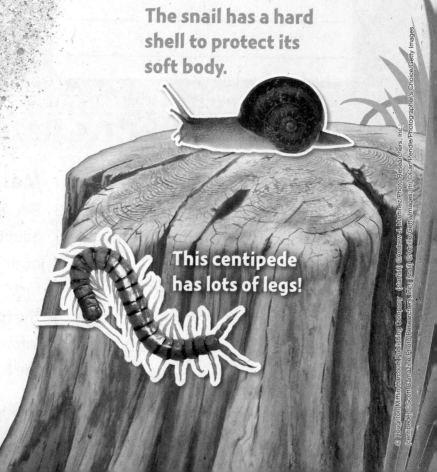

This centipede has lots of legs!

► **Place an X beneath the pictures of invertebrates.**

Ladybugs lay tiny eggs
on the undersides
of leaves.

Arthropods

There are more types of arthropods than any other type of animal. What makes them special?

Active Reading As you read these two pages, find and underline facts about insects.

Arthropods are invertebrates with jointed legs. Their bodies are divided into segments, or parts, and they have a hard, outer covering that protects them.

Insects are the largest group of arthropods. How can you tell which arthropods are insects? An insect's body has three main segments. Its head has two antennae. And it has six legs.

butterfly

walking stick

scorpion

► Find and circle these arthropods. Cross each off the list as you find it.

scorpion
butterfly
walking stick
spider
ant
tick
beetle

Spiders, scorpions, and crabs are arthropods, too. Yet they are not insects. Unlike insects, these arthropods only have two body parts. Insects always have six legs. But other kinds of arthropods have different numbers of legs.

beetle

tick

► Fill in the chart with the names of arthropods shown on these pages.

Arthropods

Insects

_____

_____

_____

Other Arthropods

_____

_____

Snails, Squids, and All the Others!

Arthropods aren't the only kind of invertebrates. What other animals are invertebrates? Look and find out!

Active Reading As you read these two pages, draw circles around the names of invertebrates.

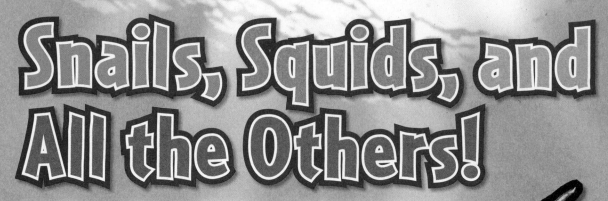

Since a squid has no bones, it can fit its body in between rocks.

Periwinkles [PER•ih•wing•kuhlz] are saltwater snails.

Brittle stars live in the ocean and in pools near the shore.

© Houghton Mifflin Harcourt Publishing Company (anemone) ©Corbis; (octopus) ©Jeff Rotman/Photo Researchers, Inc.; (slug) ©Photodisc/Getty Images; (clam) ©Andrew J. Martinez/Photo Researchers, Inc.

Do the Math!
Use Subtraction Facts

If 485 of every 500 animals are invertebrates, how many are vertebrates?

_____

_____

When this octopus hatched from its egg, it was about the size of a housefly.

Like many invertebrates, sea slugs lay eggs.

Anemones [uh•NEM•uh•neez] attach themselves to rocks or other surfaces.

A clam has a soft body with a hard shell to protect it.

Sum It Up!

When you're done, use the answer key to check and revise your work.

The blue part of each summary statement is incorrect. Write words to replace the blue parts.

1 Invertebrates are animals with backbones.

_____

_____

2 All invertebrates are arthropods.

_____

_____

3 Arthropods have one body part and jointed legs.

_____

_____

4 Insects have eight legs, two body parts, and antennae.

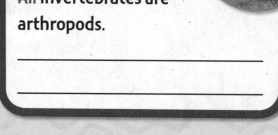

_____

_____

5 Most invertebrates give live birth to young.

_____

_____

6 Snakes and lizards are invertebrates that are not arthropods.

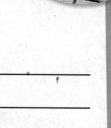

_____

_____

Answer Key: 1. without 2. Some 3. segmented bodies 4. six, three 5. lay eggs 6. Possible responses: sea snails, sea stars, jellyfish, octopuses, squids, clams

Brain Check

Lesson **3**

Name _____

Word Play

1 Use the words in the box to complete the puzzle.

Across

3. An animal without a backbone is called an _____.

5. An arthropod with six legs, three body parts, and antennae is an _____.

6. An animal with jointed legs, a segmented body, and a hard, outer covering is an _____.

7. Most invertebrates lay _____.

Down

1. All arthropods have _____ legs.

2. All arthropods have a hard, outer _____.

4. An _____ is an ocean animal with eight legs that is not an arthropod.

invertebrate*   covering   eggs

jointed   arthropod*   insect*   octopus

* Key Lesson Vocabulary

© Houghton Mifflin Harcourt Publishing Company

241

Apply Concepts

2 Look at the drawing of the scorpion. Complete the chart.

How many legs does it have?	
Does it have antennae?	
Does it have segmented body parts?	
Is it an arthropod?	
Is it an insect?	

3 Draw an arthropod of your choice.
Write what makes it an arthropod.

_____

_____

_____

_____

_____

Take It Home!

Make a poster to show different invertebrates. Group them as *arthropods* or *not arthropods*. Use labels to show the differences between the two groups.

People in Science

Meet the
Insect Scientists

**Oscar Liburd
1958–**

Liburd studies pests that attack small fruit plants.

Oscar Liburd is an entomologist. He studies insects and other pests that harm small fruit plants. He finds ways to control pests without harmful chemicals. Liburd also uses pesticides that are safer for people. In 1999, Liburd started teaching about pest control. His work today helps Florida's farmers keep pests away from their crops.

**Charles Henry Turner
1867–1923**

Charles Turner was an entomologist. He studied many kinds of insects, including ants and wasps. Turner studied honeybees, too. In 1910, he proved that honeybees can see color. The next year he proved they could also see patterns. Turner found that some ants move in circles toward their home. To honor his work with ants, scientists call this behavior "Turner's circling."

Turner showed that honeybees can see a flower's color.

The Insect Scientists

Read the timeline below. Use what you read about Liburd and Turner to fill in each blank box.

```
_____
_____
_____
_____
```

1997 Liburd graduates from the University of Rhode Island.

1910 Turner proves that honeybees can see color.

1907 Charles Turner writes about his study of ants.

```
_____
_____
_____
_____
```

Think About It!

After what year on the timeline should you add the following?

A scientist names the circles ants make when returning home "Turner's circling."

_____

Name _____

Essential Question

How Do You Classify Things?

SC.3.N.1.1 Raise questions about the natural world, investigate them...in teams through free exploration and systematic investigations... **SC.3.N.1.7** Explain that empirical evidence is...used to help validate explanations of natural phenomena. **SC.3.L.15.1** Classify animals into major groups...according to their physical characteristics and behaviors. **SC.3.L.15.2** Classify flowering and non-flowering plants into major groups such as those that produce seeds, or those like ferns and mosses that produce spores, according to their physical characteristics.

Set a Purpose

What are some ways that you can group plants or animals?

_____

_____

_____

Think About the Procedure

How will you show the different groupings on your poster?

_____

_____

_____

What characteristics will you use to classify the plants or animals?

_____

_____

_____

_____

_____

Record Your Data

Describe your categories in the space below.

Draw Conclusions

Why is classifying plants and animals by their characteristics helpful?

_____

_____

_____

Analyze and Extend

1. Compare your groupings with those of other student groups. How were they the same? How were they different? Why were they different?

_____

_____

_____

_____

2. If scientists discovered a new animal in a rain forest, what might be the first question to ask in order to classify the animal?

_____

_____

_____

3. What might make it difficult to classify some types of plants or animals using photos?

_____

_____

_____

_____

_____

_____

4. Think of other questions you might like to ask about classifying plants or animals.

_____

_____

_____

_____

_____

_____

Benchmark Review

Name _____

Multiple Choice

Identify the choice that best answers the question.

SC.3.L.15.1

1 There are many types of beetles. Which statement about beetles is true?

Ⓐ Beetles are vertebrates.

Ⓑ Beetles are insects.

Ⓒ Beetles are not insects.

Ⓓ Beetles are not invertebrates.

SC.3.L.15.1, SC.3.N.1.7

2 Look at the illustration of a jellyfish.

Which of the following features is used as evidence to classify this animal as an invertebrate?

Ⓕ tentacles

Ⓖ soft body parts

Ⓗ has a skeleton

Ⓘ does not have a backbone

SC.3.L.15.1

3 There are many different types of invertebrates. Which two invertebrates would belong in the same group?

Ⓐ jellyfish and spider

Ⓑ ant and snail

Ⓒ octopus and tick

Ⓓ beetle and walking stick

SC.3.L.15.1

4 The table below lists some of the Florida state animals.

Title	Animal
State horse	cracker horse
State fish	largemouth bass
State bird	mockingbird
State insect	zebra longwing butterfly

Which of the following animals is an arthropod?

Ⓕ cracker horse

Ⓖ largemouth bass

Ⓗ mockingbird

Ⓘ zebra longwing butterfly

SC.3.L.15.1, SC.3.N.3.2

5 Juan wants to study arthropods by making a model. Which type of animal should he make for his model?

Ⓐ

Ⓒ

Ⓑ

Ⓓ

SC.3.L.15.1, SC.3.N.1.7

6 The carpenter ant is one of the more common insects found in Florida homes. The diagram below shows the life cycle of the carpenter ant.

Life Cycle of the Carpenter Ant

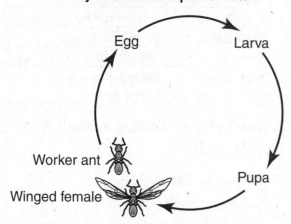

Octavio observes the diagram and says the carpenter ant is an arthropod. What could he use as evidence?

Ⓕ It hatches from an egg.

Ⓖ The female has wings and can fly.

Ⓗ The male and female look different.

Ⓘ It has a body divided into smaller parts.

SC.3.L.15.2, SC.3.N.1.1

7 Zach uses a hand lens to examine the petals of a plant. What can Zach conclude about the plant that produced the petals?

Ⓐ It is a fern plant.

Ⓑ It is a moss plant.

Ⓒ It is a flowering plant.

Ⓓ It is a nonflowering plant.

SC.3.L.15.1

8 Sungwan makes a booklet about different animals. The picture shows the animals she describes in her booklet.

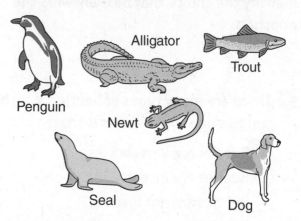

Which two of these animals are the same type of vertebrate?

Ⓕ dog and seal

Ⓖ seal and trout

Ⓗ trout and penguin

Ⓘ alligator and newt

SC.3.L.15.1

9 Dylan has a pet toad like the one in the picture. He reads a book to learn more about it. He finds out that adult toads use lungs to breathe.

Which of these animals breathes in a way that is different from the way an adult toad breathes?

Ⓐ bear

Ⓑ crocodile

Ⓒ duck

Ⓓ parrotfish

SC.3.L.15.1, SC.3.N.3.2

10 Nori is making a model of an insect. What will she need to include in the model to make it correct?

(F) wings

(G) six legs

(H) backbone

(I) eight legs

SC.3.L.15.2

11 Jamal hikes in the woods. He finds a pine cone on the hiking trail. What can Jamal conclude about the type of plant that produced the cone?

(A) It is a fern plant.

(B) It is a moss plant.

(C) It is a flowering plant.

(D) It is a nonflowering plant.

SC.3.L.15.2

12 Marty knows that two plants listed in the table below produce spores.

1	cone-bearing plants
2	fern plants
3	flowering plants
4	moss plants

Which of the following two plants produce spores?

(F) 1 and 2

(G) 1 and 3

(H) 2 and 3

(I) 2 and 4

SC.3.L.15.1

13 Sanjoy reads a book about desert animals. He thinks the most interesting animal is a mountain lion. Which other animal described in the book is the same type of vertebrate as a mountain lion?

(A) spiny lizard

(B) kangaroo rat

(C) long-eared owl

(D) monarch butterfly

SC.3.L.15.2

14 Emi sorts plants into groups. The table below shows how she groups the plants.

Group 1	Group 2
sequoia	moss
maple tree	boston fern
lily	

What would be a correct title for Group 1?

(F) flowering plants

(G) nonflowering plants

(H) seed-producing plants

(I) spore-producing plants

SC.3.L.15.1

15 On a visit to a beach, Hasna sees many sea animals. Which of the sea animals is a vertebrate?

(A) clam

(B) crab

(C) sea snail

(D) sea turtle

SC.3.L.15.2, SC.N.1.1

16 Silvio has a conifer and an apple tree in his front yard. Silvio says that the two plants are classified in two different plant groups. What is the main difference between the conifer and the apple tree?

- (F) The conifer has spores.
- (G) The conifer has stems.
- (H) The apple tree has seeds.
- (I) The apple tree has flowers.

SC.3.L.15.2

17 Neeva wants to classify the plants shown below.

1: Primrose   2: Evergreen tree

3: Apple tree   4: Oak tree

Which of the following plants will Neeva classify in the same group?

- (A) 1 and 2
- (B) 2 and 4
- (C) 1, 2, and 3
- (D) 1, 3, and 4

SC.3.L.15.2

18 Ulrich wants to classify the plants shown below based on their leaves.

1   2

3   4

Which of the following plants does not belong in this group?

- (F) 1
- (G) 2
- (H) 3
- (I) 4

SC.3.L.15.2

19 Shanika takes notes about plants during a science class. Which of the following statements is true of flowering plants?

- (A) All flowering plants produce seeds.
- (B) All flowering plants produce cones.
- (C) All flowering plants produce spores.
- (D) All flowering plants produce needles.

SC.3.L.15.1

20 Coreen has a tree house in her backyard. When she plays there, she sees many small animals. Which of the animals that she has seen is a vertebrate?

- (F) bluebird
- (G) fly
- (H) inchworm
- (I) spider

Living Things Change

Big Idea 17

Interdependence

Ten Thousand Islands region of the Everglades

I Wonder Why

This heron catches fish to eat. Other animals also eat plants or animals. Why? *Turn the page to find out.*

Here's Why Living things need energy to live, grow, and change. Animals get energy from eating plants or other animals—or both.

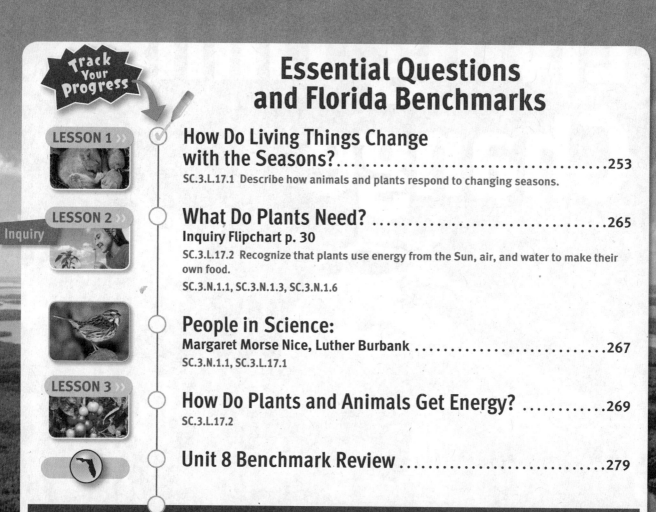

Track Your Progress

Essential Questions and Florida Benchmarks

Big Idea 17 *Interdependence*

Now I Get the Big Idea!

Essential Question

How Do Living Things Change with the Seasons?

Engage Your Brain!

Find the answer to the following question in this lesson and record it here.

This young loggerhead turtle has just hatched. During which season did this most likely happen?

_____

_____

Active Reading

Lesson Vocabulary

List terms. As you learn about each one, make notes in the Interactive Glossary.

_____

_____

Visual Aids

A picture adds information to the text that appears on the page with it. Active readers pause their reading to review the picture and decide how the information in it adds to what is provided in the text.

Spring Has Sprung!

Many places on Earth have four seasons. In those places, animals and plants change throughout the seasons of spring, summer, fall, and winter.

Active Reading As you read these pages, draw two lines under the main idea in each paragraph.

Spring is a time for growth and change. You might see tiny plants growing out of the soil. The sprouting of a seed is called **germination** [jer•muh•NAY•shuhn]. The buds on trees and shrubs open into leaves and flowers.

Animals also respond to the seasonal changes of spring. Many animals reproduce, or have their young, in spring. Perhaps you have seen young birds in a nest in the spring. In spring, some kinds of animals **migrate**, or move from one place to another. They move to find food or to reproduce.

Get growing! Many plants, such as this crocus, sprout and grow in springtime.

Caribou [KAIR·uh·boo], like some other animals, return from migration in the spring.

This mother robin feeds her young.

▶ Fill in the chart by writing details that support the main idea.

Plants and animals respond to changes in the spring.

Summertime!

With summer comes warmer weather and lots of daylight. Plants and animals grow and change in summertime.

Active Reading As you read these pages, draw a line under two details about what some living things do in summer.

In summer, many kinds of plants grow flowers. Fruits grow from parts of the flowers. The fruits contain seeds. In summer, young animals grow and become stronger. By late summer, some young animals leave the care of their parents.

These young robins grow and become stronger in the summer.

This snake has grown too big for its skin. It uses this log to help remove its old skin.

A cherry tree flowers in the spring. In summer, the flowers grow into red, ripe cherries!

This loggerhead turtle comes out of the sea to lay her eggs. The eggs hatch in about 60 days.

Many insects grow and change in the summer.

▶ What would your garden look like in summertime? Draw a picture of your garden.

Harvest Time

In fall, many plants and animals respond to cooler weather and fewer hours of daylight.

Active Reading As you read these pages, draw one line under a cause. Draw two lines under an effect.

Some trees respond to the changes of fall by dropping nuts or fruits. The leaves may also turn color and fall to the ground. Many vegetables are ready for harvest now.

Some animals respond to fall's seasonal changes, too. Some gather and store food. The fur on some animals may get thicker and change color. Other animals migrate.

Ripe fruits and vegetables are harvested, or picked, and sent to market.

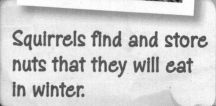

Squirrels find and store nuts that they will eat in winter.

Geese migrate to warmer places in the fall.

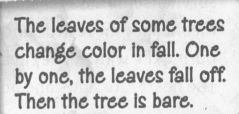

The leaves of some trees change color in fall. One by one, the leaves fall off. Then the tree is bare.

Young loggerhead turtles hatch and head for the sea.

Do the Math!
Solve a Two-Step Problem

A squirrel stores 300 nuts in a nest. It buries another 500 nuts. In winter, it eats 350 nuts. How many nuts are left?

_____

_____

Winter Days!

In many places, snow and ice cover the ground in winter. Plants and animals respond to the cold winter weather in different ways.

Active Reading As you read these two pages, draw a line under the words that describe what the photos are showing.

In many places, food is scarce in winter. To survive, some kinds of animals **hibernate**. This means they move little and use little energy during the winter. They live off stored body fat. The heart rate slows and body temperature drops.

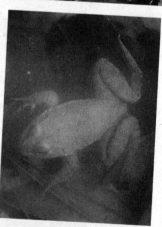

Dormice (top photo) and hedgehogs hibernate in nests. The frog is hibernating under the water of a pond. Even some insects, like these ladybugs, hibernate!

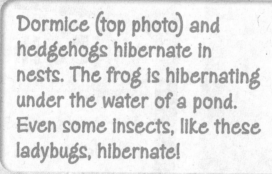

This tree has lost its leaves. It is dormant in winter.

By wintertime, most trees and bushes have lost their leaves. Without leaves, plants cannot make food for themselves. Growth slows or may even stop. These trees and bushes are said to be *dormant*. They will grow again in the spring.

▶ Compare what animals do in winter with what they do in another season.

Winter	

Sum It Up!

When you're done, use the answer key to check
and revise your work.

Complete the graphic organizer with details from the summary below.

Plants and animals change with the seasons. During spring, many seeds germinate, buds open, and many animals have their young. Summer is a time when plants and young animals grow and become strong. In fall, leaves fall from trees, crops are harvested, and animals prepare for winter. Some animals hibernate during winter, and some plants are dormant.

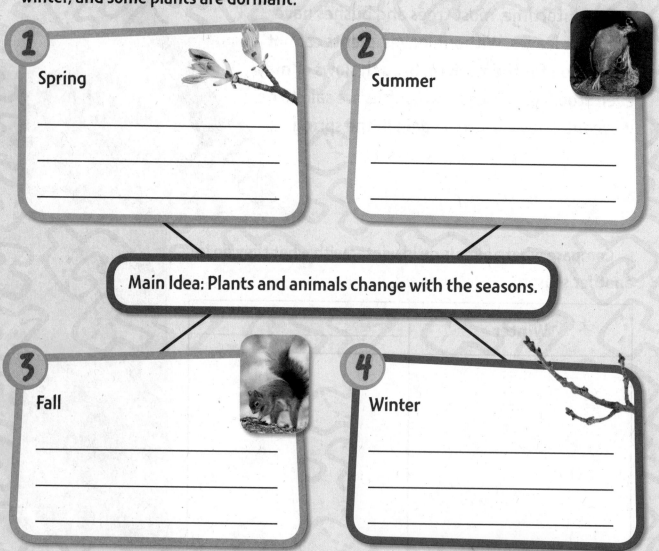

1 Spring
_____
_____
_____

2 Summer
_____
_____
_____

Main Idea: Plants and animals change with the seasons.

3 Fall
_____
_____
_____

4 Winter
_____
_____
_____

Name _____

Word Play

1 Fill in the missing letters to find each word. You will use each of the letters below.

E E E G G I I I
L M N N R T T T

1. H ___ B E ___ ___ A ___ E
2. V E ___ E ___ A B ___ ___ S
3. M ___ ___ R A ___ ___
4. G ___ R ___ I ___ A T ___ O N

Fill in the blanks with the correct word from above.

5. In winter, some animals _____ and use very little energy.

6. In springtime, _____ of many kinds of seeds takes place.

7. Animals travel from one place to another, or _____, to find food or to reproduce.

8. Many kinds of ripe fruits and _____ are harvested in the fall.

Apply Concepts

2 Look at the pictures. Write the season shown and how the plant or animal responds.

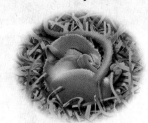  

_____ _____ _____

_____ _____ _____

3 Choose one season that you read about. Draw a picture of how a plant responds to changes in that season. Draw a picture of how an animal might respond. Then describe your pictures.

Plant Response

Animal Response

_____ _____

_____ _____

_____ _____

Take It Home!

Observe a plant or animal at home. Do you think it will respond to the coming season? If so, tell how.

264

SC.3.N.1.1 Raise questions about the natural world, investigate them... **SC.3.N.1.3** Keep records as appropriate.... **SC.3.N.1.6** Infer based on observation. **SC.3.L.17.2** Recognize that plants use energy from the Sun, air, and water to make their own food.

Name _____

Essential Question

What Do Plants Need?

Set a Purpose

What do you think you will learn from this experiment?

_____
_____
_____
_____

State Your Hypothesis

What do you predict will happen to each plant?

_____
_____
_____
_____

Think About the Procedure

Why is it important to place one plant in light and one plant in darkness and keep everything else the same?

_____
_____
_____
_____
_____

Which variable are you testing?

_____
_____

What kinds of things will you observe about the plants?

_____
_____
_____

Record Your Data

In the space below, make a data table and record your observations.

Draw Conclusions

How did the amount of light affect the plants?

_____

_____

Analyze and Extend

1. What did you observe about plant "A"? What did you observe about plant "B"?

_____

_____

_____

2. Explain how this experiment answers your hypothesis.

_____

_____

_____

3. Why did you give both plants the same amount of water?

_____

_____

_____

_____

_____

_____

4. What can you conclude about plants after this experiment?

_____

_____

_____

5. Think of other questions you would like to ask about the needs of plants.

_____

_____

_____

SC.3.N.1.1 Raise questions about the natural world, investigate them individually and in teams through free exploration and systematic investigations, and generate appropriate explanations based on those explorations. **SC.3.L.17.1** Describe how animals and plants respond to changing seasons.

Meet the Nature Scientists

Margaret Morse Nice 1883–1974

Margaret Morse Nice studied birds. For years, Nice watched the song sparrows in her yard. She kept notes on how birds mated, built nests, and raised their young. She studied how they migrate as the seasons change. Nice wrote scientific articles about her studies of birds.

Nice tagged birds with a colored band to track each bird through its life.

Luther Burbank 1849–1926

Luther Burbank wanted to improve the world's food supply. He experimented with fruits, vegetables, and flowers. To make a new kind of plant, Burbank combined two different plants. One famous plant that Burbank made was the Burbank potato. This potato was larger than other potatoes. Today it is known as the Idaho potato.

Burbank combined a plum and an apricot to make a plumcot.

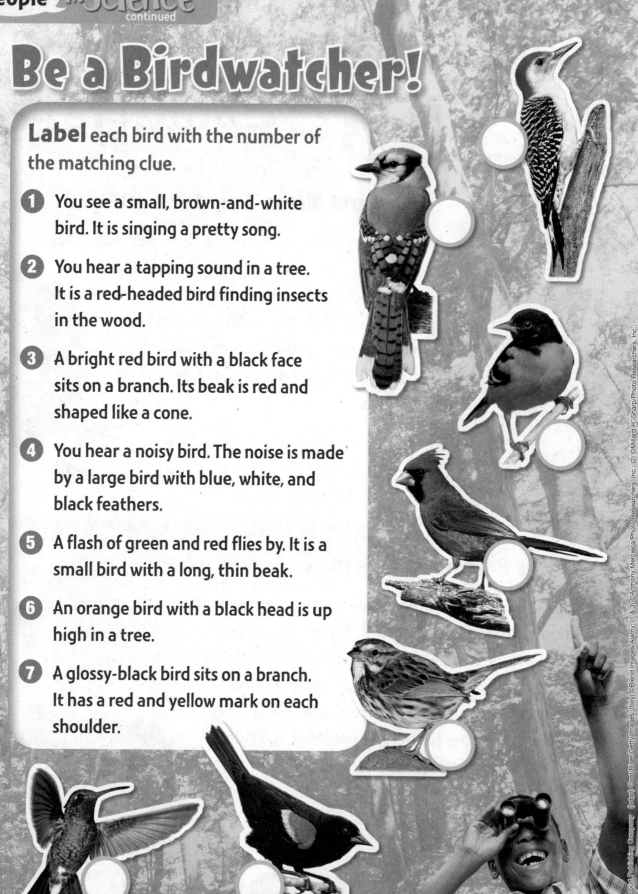

Be a Birdwatcher!

Label each bird with the number of the matching clue.

1. You see a small, brown-and-white bird. It is singing a pretty song.

2. You hear a tapping sound in a tree. It is a red-headed bird finding insects in the wood.

3. A bright red bird with a black face sits on a branch. Its beak is red and shaped like a cone.

4. You hear a noisy bird. The noise is made by a large bird with blue, white, and black feathers.

5. A flash of green and red flies by. It is a small bird with a long, thin beak.

6. An orange bird with a black head is up high in a tree.

7. A glossy-black bird sits on a branch. It has a red and yellow mark on each shoulder.

SC.3.L.17.2 Recognize that plants use energy from the Sun, air, and water to make their own food.

Essential Question

How Do Plants and Animals Get Energy?

Engage Your Brain!

Find the answer to the following question in this lesson and record it here.

What do these two animals and the grasses have in common?

_____

_____

_____

Active Reading

Lesson Vocabulary

List terms. As you learn about each one, make notes in the Interactive Glossary.

_____

_____

_____

Sequence

Many ideas in this lesson are connected by a sequence, or order, that describes the steps in a process. Active readers stay focused on sequence when they mark the transition from one step in a process to another.

Soak Up the Sun

Plants need energy to grow and reproduce. Where do you think this energy comes from?

Active Reading As you read these pages, draw one line under the source of energy for producers. Draw two lines under the products of photosynthesis that contain energy.

You eat food, such as tomatoes, to get energy. But all green plants, like these tomato plants, must produce, or make, their own food. A **producer** is a living thing that makes its own food.

The process a plant uses to make food is called **photosynthesis** [foht•oh•SIN•thuh•sis]. During photosynthesis, plants use the energy from sunlight to change water and carbon dioxide [dy•AHKS•yd], a gas in the air, into sugars. A plant uses the sugars as food for growth, or it stores them. During photosynthesis, plants give off oxygen, a gas animals need to breathe.

sunlight

Photosynthesis happens in leaves. The sun's energy is used to make sugars, which the plant uses or stores.

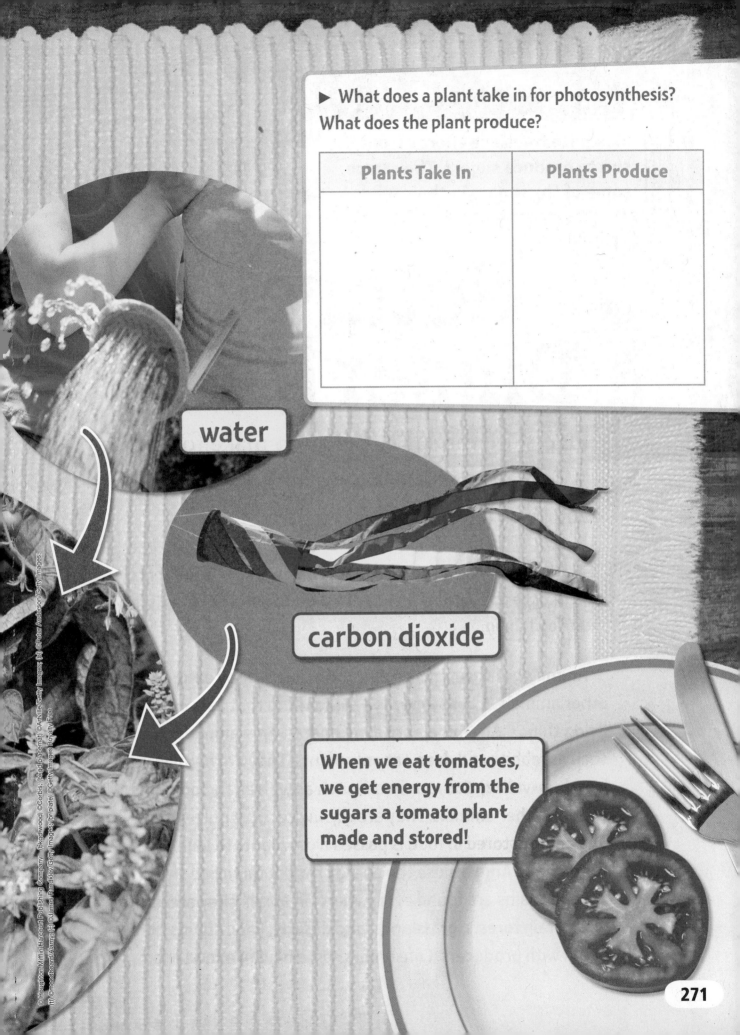

▶ What does a plant take in for photosynthesis? What does the plant produce?

Plants Take In	Plants Produce

water

carbon dioxide

When we eat tomatoes, we get energy from the sugars a tomato plant made and stored!

Mesquite trees use energy from the sun to produce sugars. They store some of the sugars in their seeds.

Nature's Dinnertime

Plants use the sun's energy to make food. Where do you think animals get the energy they need to survive?

Active Reading As you read these two pages, write numbers next to the appropriate pictures to show the order of events in the food chain.

Animals get their energy by eating plants or by eating other animals. A **consumer** is a living thing that eats other living things. All animals are consumers. Some animals, such as rabbits and deer, eat only plants. They are *herbivores* [HUR•buh•vohrz]. Some animals, such as wolves and dolphins, eat only other animals. They are *carnivores* [KAR•nuh•vohrz]. The energy stored in food is passed from plants to animals in a **food chain**. Animals use the energy from food to live and grow.

Food chains are found everywhere on Earth. They are in the ocean, rain forests, grasslands, and deserts. Food chains first begin with producers. Consumers come next in a food chain.

Kangaroo rats get energy by consuming mesquite seeds.

Rattlesnakes eat kangaroo rats to get energy.

The roadrunner is the consumer at the top of this food chain. The energy stored in food passes through the food chain to the roadrunner.

▶ Draw the missing part in the food chain. Then label the producer and the consumers.

_____

_____

_____

What's for Dinner?

You may have had corn on the cob at a picnic. Corn and other plants grown as food are known as crops.

Crops such as corn, wheat, and barley are grains grown on farms all over the United States. Crops are food for people. Crops are also food for livestock, such as cows, pigs, and chickens. Livestock are also raised as food for people. Farmers grow grains to feed livestock. The crops grown by farmers are an important part of a food chain.

Corn is a producer.

Chickens are consumers. They eat corn.

Farmers must meet the needs of plants in order for crops to grow. Crops must get plenty of air, sunlight, and water. To get water to the crops, farmers may dig long ditches. Water is pumped through the ditches to the crops. Farmers also might use sprinklers to water crops.

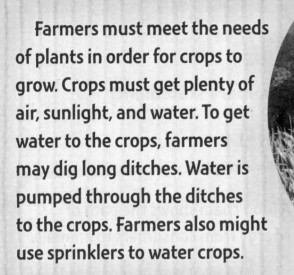

Sprinkler irrigation brings water to this crop of corn.

Do the Math!
Solve a Word Problem

It takes 8 pounds of corn to feed 40 chickens each day. How many pounds of corn does it take to feed 40 chickens in one week?

_____

_____

_____

You are a consumer who might eat corn, chicken, or both.

Sum It Up!

Find and circle the incorrect word in each summary statement. Write the correct word on the line.

1 Plants need carbon dioxide from the air, water, and oxygen to make food.

_____

2 Plants store food in the form of water.

_____

3 A living thing that eats plants or animals is a producer.

_____

4 A food chain shows the path of energy from consumers to animals.

_____

5 Crops are at the beginning of an important food grain.

_____

Answer Key: 1. oxygen; sunlight 2. water; sugars 3. producer; consumer 4. consumers; producers 5. grain; chain

Name _____

Word Play

1 Use the clues to complete the crossword puzzle.

Across

5. An animal that eats only other animals

6. A living thing that makes its own food

7. The path of energy through living things

Down

1. What plants make during photosynthesis

2. A living thing that eats other living things

3. The process plants use to make food

4. An animal that eats only plants

carnivore   herbivore

consumer*   photosynthesis*

producer*   food chain*

sugars   * Key Lesson Vocabulary

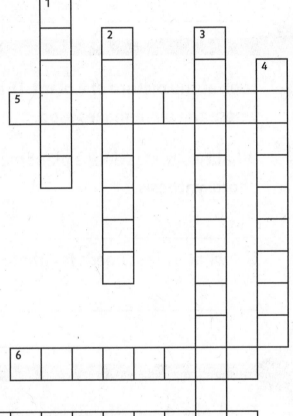

Apply Concepts

2 Look at the picture of the food chain below. Label each producer and consumer.

_____   _____   _____

3 Look at the picture of a plant. Draw an X where the plant makes food.

4 What two things does a plant make during photosynthesis?

_____

List what a plant needs for photosynthesis.

_____

_____

5 Think about some foods you eat. Draw a food chain in which you are the last link.

What crops do you eat? Make a list. Ask members of your family to add to your list. Find out where these crops come from. Are they local, or are they from far away?

Multiple Choice

Identify the choice that best answers the question.

SC.3.L.17.2, SC.3.N.1.3, SC.3.N.1.6

1 Kadim planted bean seeds in four jars with soil. He kept the jars in different places in his bedroom. For 3 weeks, he put the same amount of water into each jar. He drew these pictures to show the rest of his class how the plants looked.

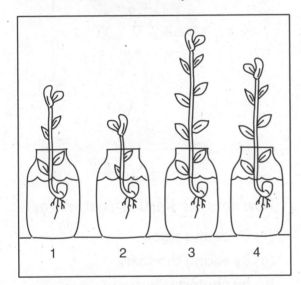

Based on the pictures, which plant was in the darkest place in Kadim's bedroom?

Ⓐ plant 1   Ⓒ plant 3

Ⓑ plant 2   Ⓓ plant 4

SC.3.L.17.2

2 Which organism is a producer?

Ⓕ grass   Ⓗ mouse

Ⓖ grasshopper   Ⓘ owl

SC.3.L.17.2

3 Julie put a plant under a growth light, watered the plant, and it grew well. Then, there was a power failure at school for one week. When school reopened, Julie's plant was the same size, but many leaves were yellow. Which sentence **best** tells what happened to the plant?

Ⓐ The plant grew well during the power failure.

Ⓑ The plant got no light during the power failure.

Ⓒ The plant did not change during the power failure.

Ⓓ The plant got too much light during the power failure.

SC.3.L.17.2

4 In a food chain, there are producers and consumers. What is the role of a producer in a food chain?

Ⓕ eat plants

Ⓖ makes its own food

Ⓗ break down dead things

Ⓘ prey on other living things

SC.3.L.17.1

5 Kobe must write a report about how some plants or animals respond to seasonal changes during the fall. Which topic should Kobe choose for his report?

Ⓐ migration   Ⓒ hibernation

Ⓑ germination   Ⓓ dormancy

SC.3.L.17.2

6 A food chain, like the one below, shows how energy moves between living things.

? → rabbit → fox

Which living thing fits **best** in the blank?

Ⓕ bird   Ⓗ carnivore
Ⓖ plant   Ⓘ herbivore

SC.3.L.17.2

7 A food chain shows how living things depend on other living things for energy. Which of the following correctly shows how energy moves through a food chain?

Ⓐ grass → oak tree → human
Ⓑ grass → chicken → human
Ⓒ human → chicken → grass
Ⓓ chicken → grass → human

SC.3.L.17.2

8 Plants get energy from the sun. Plants without sunlight will not grow. How do plants use energy from the sun?

Ⓕ to make their own food
Ⓖ to get rid of nutrients
Ⓗ to change water into sunlight
Ⓘ to change water into minerals

SC.3.L.17.2

9 All living things need certain items to live and grow. What is one thing that all living things need to live?

Ⓐ blood   Ⓒ energy
Ⓑ carbon dioxide   Ⓓ sunlight

SC.3.L.17.2, SC.3.N.1.6

10 The picture below shows a food chain in the ocean.

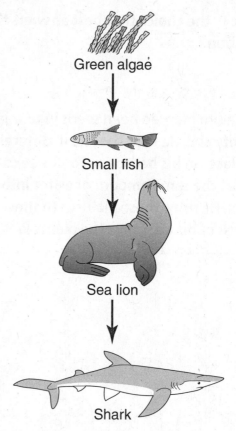

Green algae

Small fish

Sea lion

Shark

How does the small fish get energy?

Ⓕ by eating algae
Ⓖ by eating the shark
Ⓗ by photosynthesis
Ⓘ by eating the sea lion

SC.3.L.17.1

11 During the cold winter season, Ellen knows that changes happen in nature. Which of the following happens where winter is very cold?

Ⓐ Plants form flowers.
Ⓑ Most plants germinate.
Ⓒ Some animals hibernate.
Ⓓ Most animals reproduce.

SC.3.L.17.1, SC.3.N.1.1

12 During the fall, many geese migrate to places with warm temperatures. Why do geese migrate?

Ⓕ They look for snowy weather.

Ⓖ They look for food sources.

Ⓗ They look for dormant trees.

Ⓘ They look for places to hibernate.

SC.3.L.17.1

13 Mindy makes a poster about plants and animals during the spring. She wants to show how they respond to changes in the environment. Which picture does Mindy include on her poster?

Ⓐ

Ⓑ

Ⓒ

Ⓓ

SC.3.L.17.1

14 During the winter, a frog burrows in the mud to hibernate. What happens to the frog while it hibernates?

Ⓕ It uses less energy.

Ⓖ It uses more energy.

Ⓗ Its heartbeat speeds up.

Ⓘ Its body fat increases.

SC.3.L.17.1

15 Study these tree branches in the pictures below. Which tree branch would you see during the summer season?

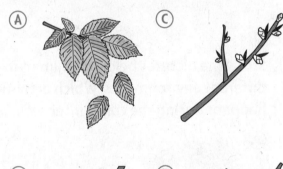

SC.3.L.17.1

16 Shanaz knows that many types of birds migrate in response to seasonal changes. During which two seasons will Shanaz see birds migrating?

Ⓕ fall and winter

Ⓖ spring and summer

Ⓗ summer and fall

Ⓘ spring and fall

SC.3.L.17.1, SC.3.N.1.3

17 In the table below, Charlotte lists some ways that animals respond to seasonal changes in the environment.

1	migrate
2	hibernate
3	reproduce
4	gather food

Which happen during the fall season?

Ⓐ 1 and 2 only

Ⓑ 1 and 3 only

Ⓒ 2 and 3 only

Ⓓ 1 and 4 only

SC.3.L.17.1

18 Study the pictures below of animals in different environments. Which activity happens during the cold winter season?

 Ⓕ   Ⓗ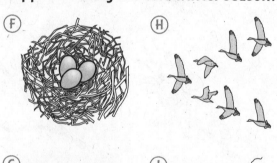

Ⓖ   Ⓘ

SC.3.L.17.1

19 Study the winter scene shown below.

In the spring, what will happen first to the tree?

Ⓐ The tree will grow fruit.

Ⓑ The tree will become dormant.

Ⓒ Flowers will bloom on the branches.

Ⓓ Buds will form on the branches.

SC.3.L.17.1, SC.3.N.1.1

20 In the table below, Adam lists reasons why birds migrate during the fall.

1	to find food
2	to gather and store food
3	to find warm weather
4	to find a place to hibernate

Which two reasons are correct?

Ⓕ 1 and 2 only

Ⓖ 1 and 3 only

Ⓗ 2 and 4 only

Ⓘ 3 and 4 only

Interactive Glossary

As you learn about each term, add notes, drawings, or sentences in the extra space. This will help you remember what the terms mean. Here are some examples.

fungi [FUHN•jee] A group of organisms that get nutrients by decomposing other organisms

A mushroom is an example of fungi.

physical change [FIHZ•ih•kuhl CHAYNJ] Change in the size, shape, or state of matter with no new substance being formed

When I cut paper in half, that's a physical change.

Glossary Pronunciation Key

With every glossary term, there is also a phonetic respelling. A phonetic respelling writes the word the way it sounds, which can help you pronounce new or unfamiliar words. Use this key to help you understand the respellings.

Sound	As in	Phonetic Respelling	Sound	As in	Phonetic Respelling
a	bat	(BAT)	oh	over	(OH•ver)
ah	lock	(LAHK)	oo	pool	(POOL)
air	rare	(RAIR)	ow	out	(OWT)
ar	argue	(AR•gyoo)	oy	foil	(FOYL)
aw	law	(LAW)	s	cell	(SEL)
ay	face	(FAYS)		sit	(SIT)
ch	chapel	(CHAP•uhl)	sh	sheep	(SHEEP)
e	test	(TEST)	th	that	(THAT)
	metric	(MEH•trik)		thin	(THIN)
ee	eat	(EET)	u	pull	(PUL)
	feet	(FEET)	uh	medal	(MED•uhl)
	ski	(SKEE)		talent	(TAL•uhnt)
er	paper	(PAY•per)		pencil	(PEN•suhl)
	fern	(FERN)		onion	(UHN•yuhn)
eye	idea	(eye•DEE•uh)		playful	(PLAY•fuhl)
i	bit	(BIT)		dull	(DUHL)
ing	going	(GOH•ing)	y	yes	(YES)
k	card	(KARD)		ripe	(RYP)
	kite	(KYT)	z	bags	(BAGZ)
ngk	bank	(BANGK)	zh	treasure	(TREZH•er)

Interactive Glossary

A

absorb [ab•SAWRB] Take in by an object (p. 137)

amphibian [am•FIB•ee•uhn] A type of vertebrate that has moist skin, begins its life in water with gills, and develops lungs as an adult to live on land (p. 226)

arthropod [AHR•thruh•pod] Animals with jointed legs and hard outer body coverings that make up the largest group of invertebrates (p. 236)

B

bar graph [BAHR GRAF] A graph using parallel bars of varying lengths to show comparison (p. 37)

C

condensation [kahn•duhn•SAY•shuhn] The process by which water vapor changes into liquid water (p. 109)

cone [KOHN] A part of some nonflowering plants where seeds form (p. 185)

consumer [kuhn•SOOM•er] A living thing that gets its energy by eating other living things (p. 272)

D

data [DEY•tuh] Individual facts, statistics, and items of information (p. 35)

data table [DEY•tuh TEY•buhl] A set of rows and columns used to record data from investigations (p. 37)

environment [en•VY•ruhn•muhnt] The things, both living and nonliving, that surround a living thing (p. 194)

E

electrical energy [ee•LEK•trih•kuhl EN•er•jee] A form of energy that can move through wires (p. 126)

evaporation [ee•vap•uh•RAY•shuhn] The process by which liquid water changes into water vapor (p. 108)

evidence [EV•uh•duhns] Information, collected during an investigation, to support a hypothesis (p. 35)

energy [EN•er•jee] The ability to make something move or change (p. 124)

experiment [ek•SPAIR•uh•muhnt] A test done to see if a hypothesis is correct or not (p. 11)

Interactive Glossary

F

flower [FLOW•er] The part of a flowering plant that enables it to reproduce (p. 184)

flowering plant [FLOW•er•ing PLANT] A plant that produces seeds within a fruit (p. 214)

food chain [FOOD CHAYN] The flow of food energy in a sequence of living things (p. 272)

force [FAWRS] A push or a pull (p. 70)

G

gas [GAS] A form of matter that has no definite shape or volume (p. 102)

germinate [JER•muh•nayt] To start to grow (a seed) (p. 197)

germination [jer•muh•NAY•shuhn] The sprouting of a seed (p. 254)

graduated cylinder [GRAJ•oo•ay•tid SIL•in•der] A container marked with a graded scale used for measuring liquids (p. 21)

gravity [GRAV•ih•tee] A force that pulls two objects toward each other (p. 70)

infer [in•FER] To draw a conclusion about something (p. 6)

H

heat [HEET] Energy that moves from warmer to cooler objects (p. 156)

insect [IN•sekt] A type of animal that has three body parts and six legs (p. 236)

hibernate [HY•ber•nayt] To go into a deep, sleeplike state for winter (p. 260)

invertebrate [in•VER•tuh•brit] An animal without a backbone (p. 234)

hypothesis [hy•PAHTH•uh•sis] A possible answer to a question that can be tested to see if it is correct (p. 10)

investigation [in•ves•tuh•GAY•shuhn] A study that a scientist does (p. 9)

K

kinetic energy [kih•NET•ik EN•er•jee] The energy of motion (p. 124)

L

liquid [LIK•wid] A form of matter that has a volume that stays the same but has a shape that can change (p. 102)

M

mammal [MAM•uhl] A type of vertebrate that has hair or fur and feeds its young with milk from the mother (p. 229)

mass [MAS] The amount of matter in an object (p. 86)

matter [MAT•er] Anything that takes up space (p. 85)

mechanical energy [muh•KAN•ih•kuhl EN•er•jee] The total potential and kinetic energy of an object (p. 124)

microscope [MY•kruh•skohp] A tool that makes an object look several times bigger than it is (p. 19)

migrate [MY•grayt] To travel from one place to another and back again (p. 254)

P

photosynthesis [foht•oh•SIN•thuh•sis] The process that plants use to make food (p. 270)

N

nonflowering plant [non•FLOW•er•ing PLANT] Plants that reproduce without making flowers (p. 216)

physical property [FIZ•ih•kuhl PRAHP•er•tee] Anything that you can observe about an object by using one or more of your senses (p. 85)

nutrient [NOO•tree•uhnt] A material in the soil that helps plants grow and stay healthy (p. 178)

potential energy [poh•TEN•shuhl EN•er•jee] Energy of position or condition (p. 124)

O

observe [uhb•ZURV] To use your senses to gather information (p. 6)

predict [pri•DIKT] Use observations and data to form an idea of what will happen under certain conditions (p. 8)

Interactive Glossary

producer [pruh•DOOS•er] A living thing that makes its own food (p. 270)

reptile [REP•tyl] A type of vertebrate that has dry skin covered with scales (p. 226)

R

reflect [rih•FLEKT] To bounce off (p. 138)

S

seed [SEED] A structure that contains a young plant and its food supply, surrounded by a protective coat (p. 184)

refract [rih•FRAKT] To bend light as it moves from one material to another (p. 140)

shadow [SHAD•oh] A dark area that forms when an object blocks the path of light (p. 137)

reproduce [ree•pruh•DOOS] To make more living things of the same kind (p. 184)

solid [SAHL•id] A form of matter that has a volume and a shape that both stay the same (p. 102)

spore [SPAWR] A reproductive structure made by some plants, including mosses and ferns, that can grow into a new plant (p. 218)

temperature [TEM•per•uh•cher] A measure of how hot or cold something is (pp. 23, 90, 157)

star [STAR] A hot ball of glowing gases that gives off energy (p. 53)

V

variable [VAIR•ee•uh•buhl] The one thing that changes in an experiment (p. 11)

sun [SUHN] The star closest to Earth (p. 52)

vertebrate [VER•tuh•brit] An animal with a backbone (p. 224)

T

telescope [TEL•uh•skohp] A device people use to observe distant objects with their eyes (p. 58)

volume [VAHL•yoom] The amount of space that matter takes up (p. 88)

Index

Index

orchids, 214
Food chain, 272, 277
  crops in, 274, 276
Force, 70–75
  of rocket, 72
Forceps, 18, 27. *See also*
  Science tools
Franklin, Benjamin,
  133–134
Freezing, 104, 115
Friction, 163

G

Gas, 102, 107–109, 111–112
Germination, 197, 203
  in spring, 254, 263
Gold, 95
Graduated cylinder, 21,
  26–27. *See also* **Science
  tools**
  to measure volume, 89
Gravity, 69, 74–76, 203
  force, 70–71, 74–76
  growth of roots, 200–201
  growth of stem, 200–201
  launch of rocket, 73
  pull, 70–71, 75, 200
  ways to overcome, 72–76

H

Hail, 105
Hand lens, 17–19, 26–27,
  64. *See also* **Science tools**
Hang glider, 73
Hardness, 85

Heat, 127, 131–132, 156,
  160, 164, 166. *See also*
  Energy
  draw conclusions, 168
  fire, 162
  flow of, 157–159, 164
  producing, 162–163
  record data, 167
  sources, 161
Herbivores, 272, 277
Hibernate, 260
  dormice, 260
  hedgehog, 260
  leopard frog, 260
  in winter, 260–264
Hyacinth bulbs, 197
Hypothesis, 10–13

I

Infer, 6, 12–14, 64
Inquiry Skills
  classify, 212–213, 245–246
  communicate, 36–39
  compare, 41, 96
  draw conclusions, 11, 16,
    30, 42, 64, 66, 98, 100,
    114, 148, 168, 192, 246,
    266
  experiment, 11–13
  hypothesize, 10–13
  infer, 6, 12–14, 64
  measure, 21–23, 26–27,
    29–30, 87, 89–91
  observe, 6, 13–14
  plan investigation, 10
  predict, 8, 10, 12–13

record data, 10, 15, 25, 29,
  33–37, 39–41, 63, 65,
  97, 99, 113, 147, 167,
  191, 245, 266
  sequence, 12, 177, 269
  use models, 12–16
  variables, identify 11–14
Insects, 236–237
  ant, 237
  beetle, 237
  butterfly, 236–237
  entomologist, 243
  honeybee, 243–244
  ladybug, 235
  in summer, 257
  walking stick, 236–237
Insect Scientists, 244
Inventors, 67, 133–134
Invertebrates, 234–235,
  240
  anemone, 239
  arthropods, 236–237
  brittle star, 238
  centipede, 234
  clam, 239
  ladybug, 235
  octopus, 239
  periwinkle, 238
  sea slug, 239
  sea star, 234
  snail, 234
  squid, 238
  worm, 234
Investigation, 9
  draw conclusions, 16
  experiment, 11
  plan investigation, 10

Index

Index